Also by Hubert Germain-Robin

Traditional Distillation Art & Passion

THE MATURATION
OF
DISTILLED SPIRITS

Vision & Patience

❧

Hubert Germain-Robin

Published by White Mule Press
distilling.com; whitemulepress.com

Printed in the United States of America

ISBN 978-0-9968277-0-6

Cover photo by Craig Lee, *San Francisco Chronicle*/Polaris.

TABLE OF CONTENTS

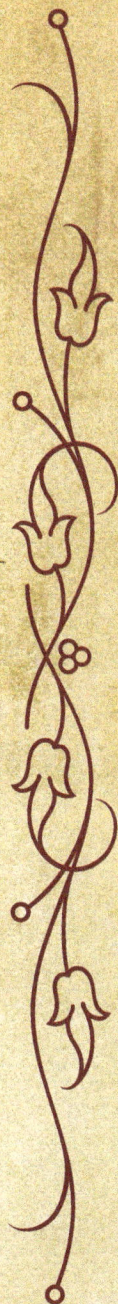

FOREWORD

The Maturation of Distilled Spirits: Vision and Patience marks the first time, to my knowledge, that the art of spirits aging and blending has been written about in any great depth in the English language. Even when the topic has been addressed, it is usually given a cursory treatment that describes the function of the oak barrel, and then jumps directly to explaining the proofing process of reducing a spirit from cask to bottling strength.

Oddly, precious little has been said or written about what happens in the life of a spirit in the intermediary stages it goes through when it is fresh from the still and goes into the barrel until bottling time. It is as if there is an unspoken belief that once the new make spirit is placed in the barrel, it should be tucked away and left alone undisturbed until someone finally decides to awaken it from its slumber. Yet, given that a distillate can age in a barrel anywhere from one minute to 50 or 60 years, this long period in the life of a spirit is absolutely crucial to appreciate and understand if one intends to ever produce a high quality product.

No one is more qualified to impart this ancient knowledge and wisdom than Hubert Germain-Robin, an 11th generation Cognac maker with over 40 years of production experience in both the Old and New World.

The art of spirits maturation is often referred to as *élevage* in the French brandy and wine world. It literally means to raise or educate a distilled spirit as if it were a one's own child. To fully capture this concept, imagine that a spirit is conceived through the marriage of the simple sugars from a raw ingredient and yeast during the fermentation process. It then gestates in a copper pot still womb as it transforms from liquid into vapor, and is finally born as it re-condenses back to liquid, when it trickles out the still parrot into the cradle of a receiving tank.

Just after birth, however, this new-make spirit "baby" is quite rough and raw. It has potential to eventually become a sophisticated and refined adult, but it will require much supervision to lead it from the enfant stage through adolescence and finally on to maturity. This marks the period of *élevage*, and is where the skills of the Cellar Master and Master Blender will shape the upbringing of the barrels containing the baby spirit.

This individual will be both parent and teacher to the spirits by matching them with oak barrels that will tease out their finest qualities. He or she must also monitor the aging environment of the barrels, and if it is either too dry or too humid, will move the barrels to more appropriate maturation conditions. He or she will need vision and experience to see if the spirit should be released as a younger product, or if it is destined for the kind of long-term aging that will give it great complexity and harmony. The job of a Cellar Master/Master Blender is also that of a steward, constantly monitoring and tasting the barrels in the aging warehouses to insure barrel health and consistency of quality for generations to come. It is a job that requires much passion, patience, time and commitment, with a realization that the work is never complete.

I first became aware of Hubert Germain-Robin's work in 2006. A few years prior, I had developed a strange but strong passion to learn everything I could about distilled spirits and their production. As a recent law school graduate, my devotion to studying all about spirits—for better or worse—was much greater than my dedication to pass the bar exam. Even so, in anticipation of following a tedious family tradition into the world of law, I took a job in the library of a large labor and employment firm in a soulless high-rise building deep in bowels of the San Francisco financial district while I nervously awaited the bar exam results.

During this time, one crisp autumn evening I attended a fund-raiser for the mentoring and tutoring of adolescent girls. I wandered up to a table that was offering small tastes of Alambic style brandies. The intense young lady working the table, Adrienne, explained that these spirits were very special, as they had been produced by a Cognac distiller who had come to California in 1982 to make brandy using age-old, hand-crafted techniques to produce them. After one taste, I was hooked! I could literally taste the passion in these brandies made with high quality varietal wine grapes. The experience ignited my own deep passion for how to make spirits that have depth, complexity, and finesse, and I have never looked back.

Soon thereafter, I quit my job at the law firm, traveled through Morocco, Spain, and Mexico in order to find myself, and then exactly a year after that fateful fund-raising event I was working at the much-celebrated Germain-Robin brandy distillery. By the time I arrived, Hubert had already moved on to become an International Master Distilling/Blending Consultant. However, I would later meet him in person after I had moved on from my own work at the distillery in order to consult, and we developed a friendship and mentorship based on a mutual love of well-made spirits.

Through his infinite experience and wisdom, Hubert has instilled in me a keen sense of just how significant it is to pay attention to every detail of a spirit's maturation—and indeed, to every aspect of the production process, from the grapes, grain or cane in a field, all the way down to the bottling line.

In order to make a world-class, high quality aged distilled spirit, great care and patience is required during the maturation, warehousing and blending phase. This means not cutting corners even when it would be more convenient to do so. It means using only high quality cooperage, knowing when to transfer your spirits from one barrel to another (when legally permissible), paying careful attention to having the right climatic conditions of the aging cellar or warehouse, having the discipline to implement a slow water reduction program into your production schedule for double distilled products, knowing the fundamentals of good cellar management, and understanding when it is appropriate or not to use traditional blending tools such as caramel, sugar syrup, and boisé, etc.

Perhaps most importantly, though, Hubert has taught me that in order to create high quality distilled spirits, one must always keep an open mind and have a sense of humility. It is truly humbling to see a man with such great experience and a wealth of knowledge express that he is always learning new things about the art of distillation, maturation and blending.

Finally, the ancient Greeks spoke of the concept or virtue of areté, meaning "excellence," or "being the very best you can be." I invite you the reader to learn from Hubert's deep wisdom and to adopt this virtue in striving to become an ever better distiller or blender. It is my sincere hope that those within our industry in the Americas will drink deeply from a well of experience in maturation, cellaring and blending that is centuries old, and push the envelop by applying it to New World products in order to create distilled spirits of ever greater quality.

Spirits of excellence, after all, do not just happen—they are painstakingly made.

Nancy Fraley
Maturation & Blending Consultant
Berkeley CA, 2015

PREFACE

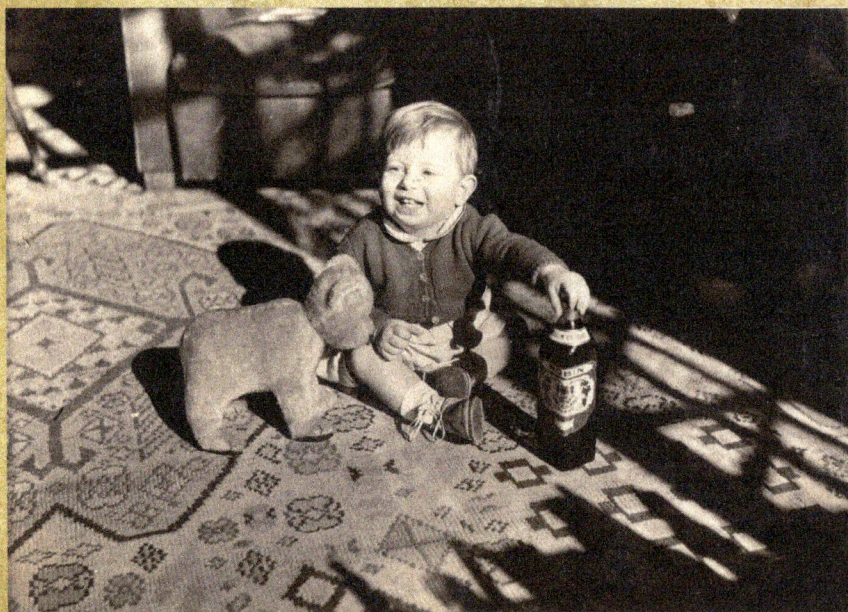

in the beginning...

After years of education and apprenticeship in Cognac on traditional and strict methods of production, I came to America to explore new distilling and aging possibilities. I had to relearn and adapt my knowledge to completely new parameters, such as microclimates, geology, grape varietals, fermentation profiles, distillation and the complexity of maturing and aging. Each move had to be rethought to envision the future of these alambic brandies. I was excited by the challenge and seized the opportunity to be imaginative with new territories.

It is a dream for any craft distiller/blender to be confronted with such a challenge. I feel blessed to have been born in the Cognac region; to grow up in my ancestral environment, and have the support from the Prulho (alambic pot still manufacturer) and Vicard (cooper) families. I have also received a warm welcome from the community of Mendocino County, California, with special mention to the people in the wine industry. My wife Carole and I trusted our lucky star: Our new home turned out to be the perfect place to make world-class spirits.

Now, enter the cellar master and the master blender. In small companies, the same person performs most of those tasks. In large companies, those tasks are much more divided, even if each person knows all aspects of production. The goal is to transform the clear liquid into gold.

The cellar master's task is to manage all the movements in the cellar, to nurture the eaux de vie (EDVs), and to develop them as different entities. The cellar master needs to keep age factors in mind: short term—3 to 5 years; medium term—6 to 15 years; and long term—more than 15 years. He will have important decisions to make, such as type of oak, toastage and duration in the new barrels, along with speed of reduction, style of blends, and more.

Eaux-de-Vie et Bouilleurs, Jean-Louis Neveu

After the grower
After the fermenter
After the distiller

The master blender needs to properly integrate all the pieces of the puzzle to attain balance, harmony and complexity. In this regard, he is also a buyer in conjunction with the cellar master for new EDV or older spirits to renew the stock, to add another appellation or other varietals, and to prepare his company for the future.

Both the master blender and master distiller have the important role of evaluating the inventory yearly, and deciding the future of each barrel and lot. Are the contents mature enough to be part of a blend? Do they have the personality to be released as a single varietal, a single vineyard, or will they spend many more years in barrels to reach their "quintessence"? Have they already attained their peaks of maturity and will they need to spend the rest of their lives in glass demijohns in paradise?

The expertise of the master blender and cellar master derives from many years of experience and is the heart and soul of a spirits company. Their decisions impart the style and the quality of their brown spirits for a long time. Their training is long and progressive. Their knowledge should cover all aspects of production—from growing, to crushing and fermentation, distillation, and all aspects of the aging process. Their goal is an accord between aromas achieved by patterns of recognition instead of pure memorization.

To put things in perspective regarding time: "You make brown spirits for your sons and daughters and drink the ones from your father."

I invite you, the reader, to share my passion and my experience. My ambition is simply to present some of the possibilities that distillers have after refining and concentrating the spirits' essences by careful distillation. I accomplished my work through intuition and patience; by learning and experimenting but, above all, with the guidance of recognized masters who paved my way by sharing their knowledge and know-how with me.

CHAPTER 1

d'après MEUSEL et al., 1965; *Journal International des Sciences de la Vigne et du Vin*

Oak Sources

Oak first appeared on earth a little over 65 million years ago. Today, oak trees grow to maturity in the temperate zones, but many of the species are shrubs and quite unsuited to barrel production. There are more than 500 species of *Quercus* in the Northern Hemisphere alone, plus another 86 natural hybrids in the USA.

In the USA, two regions are the principal source of oak: The Ozarks, and the Appalachian mountain chain, which has a history of depletion, then re-establishment, due to the level of rainfall during climate changes. These two regions represent a rich source of flavorful extractives and high oxidation potential. *Quercus alba*, commonly known as American oak, is the dominant white oak throughout the USA. Other sub-species occur more frequently in other regions. For example, sub-species such as *Querqus makocarpe*—the bur oak—is found in valley bottoms, and *Quercus muehlenbergii*—the chinkapin oak—occurs on well drained slopes.

In France, the situation is quite different. French forests are managed by the Office National des Forêts (ONF). The two species, *Quercus robur* and *Quercus petrae*, are found in nearly equal proportions, although the former is becoming the more abundant. Since the beginning of the 20th century, forest inventories have been thriving and expanding.

French production of oak has increased to 325,000 cubic yards,

Quercus robur pedunculata

Quercus petraea, or sessilis

Quercus alba, or American White Oak

producing about 500,000 barrels of different sizes per year. Half of that is for export to different parts of the world.

Origins of the Oak Trees

The essence and the *terroir* of the oak are crucial for the aging of spirits. The grain tightness depends mainly on soil moisture retention, available soil nutrients and the density of the forests.

Quercus robur pedunculata

Quercus robur grows mainly in the rich soil of the Limousin forest, located in the center of France. Being of large diameter, these trees offer large grain, which is more porous, resulting in faster extraction of wood compounds during the maturation process, and yielding complex structure and ample tannins.

The *Quercus robur*, which grows in Russia and in the Limousin forests in France, prefer deep fertile soils, deep loam and chalk. Full sunlight is crucial to their full development.

Quercus petraea, or sessilis

Quercus petraea, or sessile oak, grows in light, sandy, loamy and rocky soils. They tend to be lean and tall, with tight grain, so there is a slower extraction during the maturation of a spirit. The trees are taller, straighter, and older due to close planting and the shadowy light of the forests. They take between 100 to 150 years to reach maturity and can be found in forests such as the Tronçais, Allier, Vosges, and in Eastern Europe.

Quercus alba, or American White Oak

Quercus alba tends to be less tannic than the European species and is quite rich in vanillins and lactones. They offer characteristic aromas of coconut and vanilla, bringing softness to distillates. Sometimes, an aroma of green olive is present when the staves are not air-dried long enough and the toastage is too light. New barrels are used primarily for bourbon and other American whiskeys, with the used barrels finding a secondary market for the aging of other brown spirits, such as Scotch, rum and Tequila.

Tree growth is faster than its European counterparts, maturing in 60 to 80 years. Although the eastern two-thirds of the United States possesses *Quercus alba*, the best trees are grown in the Ozarks, where the growing conditions have rocky soils, thick undergrowth, and produce more extracts compared to trees grown in northern climates or in the deep south.

Quercus garyana, or Oregon Oak

Oregon oak can be found from southern California to southwestern British Columbia. It does have a beautiful grain similar to a European oak, but needs to be well seasoned, and attention should be paid to the straightness of the grain. Irregular grain can cause splitting and leaking; consequently, the staves should be thicker than with other American white oaks. Typical characteristics include savory spices and smoke.

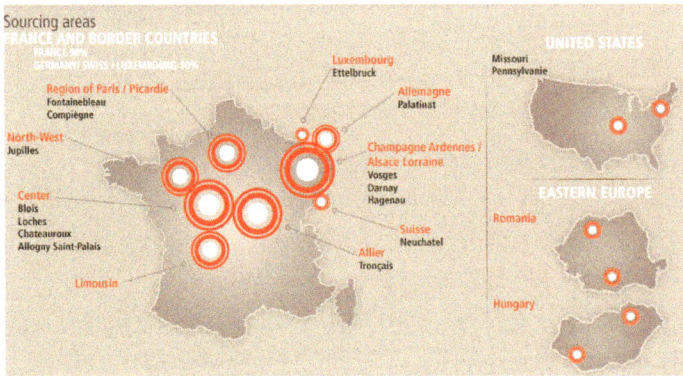

Courtesy: Tonnellerie Vicard

French Forests

The oak forests of France are quite diversified in terms of soil conditions, micro-climates, density of trees, and locations in which they are found. Below is a partial list in alphabetic order, either by departments, regions, or cities: Allier, Bercé, Bertrange, Bitche, Bretagne, Citeaux, Darney, Dordogne, Fontainebleau and Blois, Gers, Jupille, Jura, Montlezun and Monguilhem (Armagnac), Limousin, Nevers, Pyrenees, Troncais and Vosges forests.

Limousin (*Q. robur*)—principal source for spirits with its wide-grained wood of around 8 grains per inch.

Color—dark yellow

Growth—large, slow, with wide grains

Allier (*Q. sessilis*)

Color—clear yellow

Growth—high, fast, with fine grain

Courtesty: Tonnellerie Vicard

American (*Q. alba*)

Color—off white/cream

Growth—faster growth, fine grain

Armagnac

200 years ago, the Armagnac region had 155 barrel-makers; now, there are only three.

Only 10% of the oak used in the Armagnac region comes from the local forests of Montlezun and Monguilhem, which grow black oak (*Quercus silicus*). The Limousin forests provide 85% of the oak, while 5% comes from other parts of France and Europe.

Cognac

About 70% of the staves used in Cognac barrels are wide-

Courtesy: American Distilling Institute

grained oak from the Limousin forests; the remaining 30% are fine-grained oak from the center of France—Allier and Tronçais forests.

Barrels in America

A century ago, there were thousands of coopers in America. Now, only 25 barrelmakers are in operation. However, there are now more than 700 craft distillers in the USA, and rapidly approaching 1,000, compared to the early 1980s, when there were only five in production.

American whiskeys, with the exception of corn, have to be aged in new charred oak casks, resulting in a deficit of barrels for their production. There is even a shortage of barrels in the secondary market for used barrels.

The charring process for barrels imparts strong caramelized flavors from the wood sugar with an intense smoky character, creating powerful masking flavors. The other effect of charring is the disappearance of the terroir, or character coming from microclimates, air quality, and minerals, which reduces complexity and upsets the balance.

These states and regions are the main sources of oak for barrels: Arkansas, Iowa, Minnesota, Missouri, the Ozark Mountains, Pennsylvania, Tennessee, Oregon and Wisconsin.

The American cooperage industry produces about 1 million barrels of 55-gallon capacity per year, most of which are destined for aging bourbon.

Japanese Oak (*Quercus mongolica*)

Mizunara oak has been used for the Japanese whiskey industry since the 1930s. The casks are highly prone to leaking and damage, since the oak is soft and very porous. As a consequence, the aging process has been modified; therefore, bourbon and sherry casks are now being used for maturation. The whiskeys are then transferred to mizunara barrels to gain their unique profile of flavors, such as vanilla, honey, flower blossoms, pear, apple, clove, nutmeg and spices, plus sandalwood and coconut aromas. In comparison with American oak, Japanese oak has slightly more "cis-oak" lactones, which are responsible for coconut aromas, and much more "trans-oak" lactones, resulting in stronger and more persistent aromas which are complimentary to grain spirits.

Other Oak Regions

Russia

Quercus sessilis is from the region of Adyghe near the Black Sea on the 45th parallel. It is very similar to the oak from the French forests of Allier and Tronçais in that it grows very tall with tight-grained oak. They also have *Quercus robur*, similar to the Limousin forests but the tannins are more intense than the French, with elegant and sweet aromas.

Poland

Quercus sessilis, has cardamom aromas.

Serbia & Hungary

Quercus sessilis produces a wide variety of spice notes.

Italy

Fraimelto, which is fine-grained with light tannins and lots of finesse.

Bulgaria

Quercus sessilis. The forest of the Southern Balkans produce mostly slow growth Sessile oak.

Spain

Sessile oak from the northern region of Galicia.

Czech/Moravian/Carpatian/Romanian

Sessile oak

CHAPTER 2

Selection of Oak Trees for Barrels

The Forests

The forester is in charge of watching and selecting the oak trees. His primary mission is to constantly evaluate the progression of each individual tree with respect to its maturity, development and shape.

Cutting the trees after the full moon is always preferable, as the sap goes down from the tree during the waning moon.

Jean-Charles Vicard, of the Vicard Tonnellerie in Cognac, describes the expertise and role of the forester. "He is able to read through the bark of oak trees up to 45 feet to determine the number of barrels he will be able to make from a standing tree wrapped with bark." Vicard is a wood engineer with more than 25 years of experience in the forest. This science has been passed down for centuries from generation to generation.

The tasting of wines or spirits allows the taster to fill himself with the quality, the aromas and the structure of the sample. With the oak, the process is identical: When the experts drill at the base of the oak trees and then chew on the chips, they verify its texture and taste, and make sure they are not affected by diseases such as mold or infested with insects before cutting them.

The trees that are estimated to be ready to buy are between 180 to 300 years old, with a diameter between 2 to 3 1/3 feet (60 to

100 centimeters). For example, the Tronçais forest, situated in the center-east of France, is planted in mature timber, meaning that when the trees are small, the foresters of the Office National des Forêts (ONF) leave the seedlings close to each other so that the trees are searching upward for light. This results in straight trunks of 26 to 50 feet (8 to 15 meters) high before the first branch. The straight-growing trees allow the cooper to select the length of the logs more accurately and efficiently, from which the staves will be split.

You can find significant differences of porosity in the same area of a forest, even with identical rings. This variance influences the wood's structure; the density (frequency and dimension of the pores) and the permeability (the ability to let liquid penetrate through the anatomic structure in function of the pressure and the orientation of the grain). The tightness of the grain controls the oxygenation by allowing gas exchange between the inside and outside of the barrel, but also by monitoring the speed and level of extraction from the oak.

There are three primary types of grain orientation:
· Transverse (across at a right angle)
· Longitudinal with radial rays (radius in the length)
· Longitudinal with tangential rays

The width of the growing rings is determined by the speed of growth.

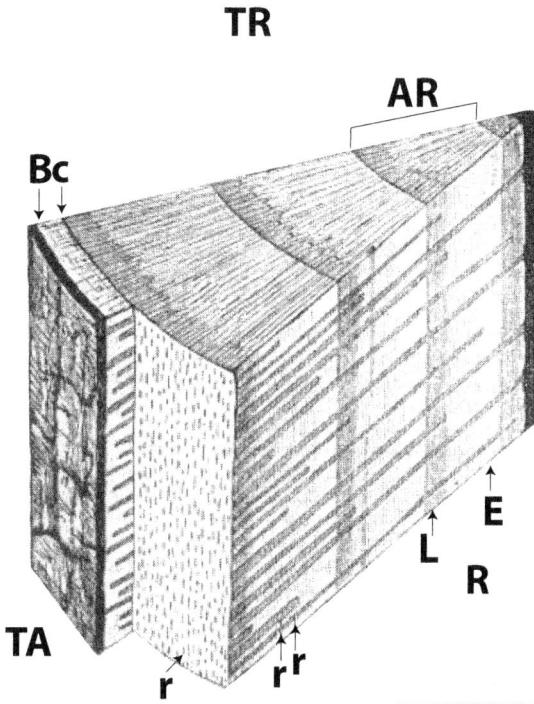

TR

AR

Bc

TA

r   rr

L   E

R

TR: transversal section
R: radial section
TA: tangential section
B: bark
c: cambium
r: radial ray
AR: annual ring
E: earlywood
L: latewood

Tyloses occurences

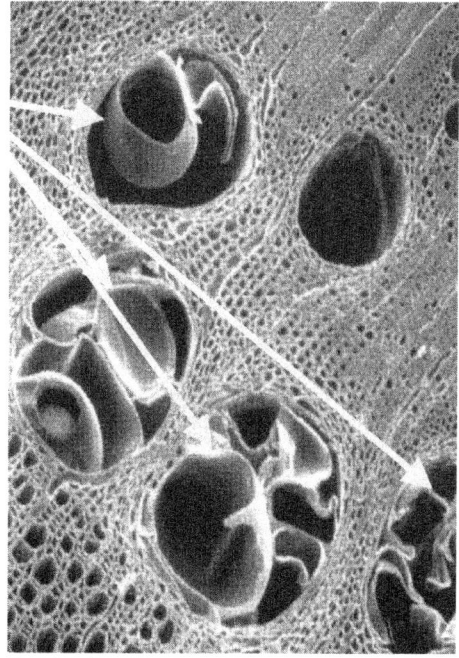

French oak structure—micro and macro from
International Barrel Symposium, ISC

CHAPTER 3

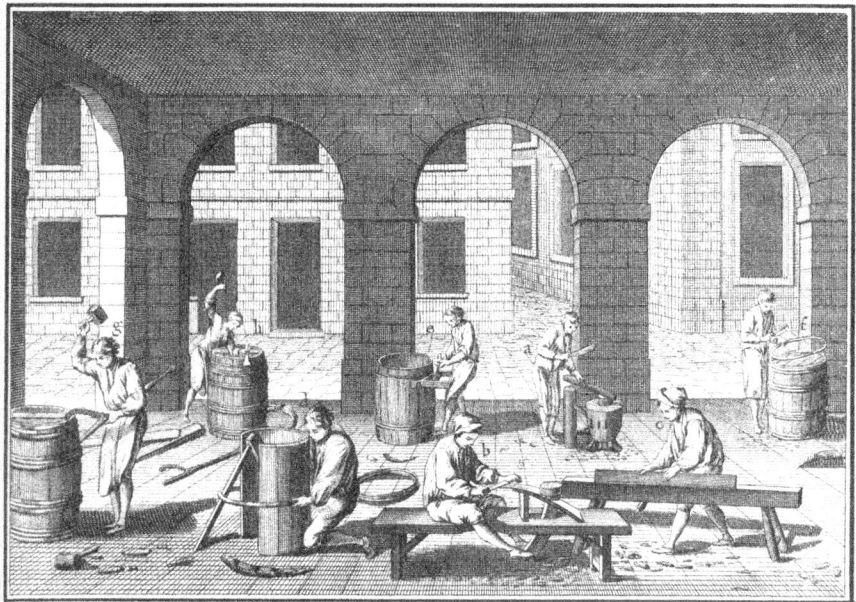

Encyclopedie de Diderot

Barrels

History

Assyrians used palm wood barrels to replace amphorae in transporting wine from Armenia to Mesopotamia and Babylon because of the fragility of the ceramic vessels, which often broke, resulting in expensive losses.

Many types of wood have since been used for the aging and transportation of wines, liquors, and spirits such as acacia, beech wood, chestnut, locust, mulberry, hickory, redwood and willow.

Oak Properties

The strength, hardness, flexibility and serviceability of the double arch construction make the barrel a perfect container; plus, they are very easy to move from place to place. The low porosity, favorable tannin extraction and their oxygenation allow a genuine intracellular respiration by capillary penetration of the spirits through the wood. The oak is also a good thermal insulator, which mitigates temperature fluctuation in the cellar.

Terroir

The composition varies among the different species and hybrids. This variability results in different aspects: anatomic, physical, mechanic, chemical and genetic, but also in function of cultivation methods and the interactions of their growing conditions. Like all plants, the oak trees acquire a particular terroir, depending on their closeness to one another, their placement in the forests (i.e., the edge or middle of the forest), natural drainage, depth and composition of the soils, elevation, direction of the wind, pluviosity (rainfall), proximity of rivers, lakes, oceans and, unfortunately, pollution.

Courtesy: Tonnellerie Vicard

Characteristics

French and European oak (*Q. robur* and *sessile*), being physiologically different in structure compared to American oak, need to be split by hand when making the staves. This is one of the primary reasons why French oak barrels cost more than American oak barrels.

American oak (*Q. alba*) is richer in tyloses, which seal the pores and tubes of the wood. This means that American oak is less porous than the French species. Being more impermeable, the American oak can be sawn into staves rather than hand-split along the wood's grain to prevent leakage. Sawing the oak into staves means that coopers can use more than twice as much wood from each log in the stave's production.

Nowadays, lasers enable barrel-makers to follow the medullary ray with amazing precision for splitting the wood. Consequentially, this reduces waste to a minimum, and also avoids the cross grain-cutting course of potential leaks.

Construction of a Barrel

After the selection in the forest is made and the trees are cut according to their shape and diameter, they are split into bolts of different lengths along the vertical grain. They are hand-split first into halves, then quarters, and finally sawed into staves of 3 to 5 inches wide and about 1 inch thick.

The staves are stored outside in a latticed stack with space between the rows to allow them to dry down from 80% moisture to approximately 14 to 18% moisture. During two to three years, the seasoning of the staves occurs under the yearly climatic cycle. Biochemical, physical, and mechanical reactions are developing, and provide complex natural flavors, which are beneficial to spirits.

After the staves have been planed to form the outer convex curve (to make the inner surface concave), the barrel-maker can put them in a rose.

Courtesy: Tonnellerie Vicard

Construction of a Barrel

BARREL MANUFACTURE
the logs are cut to the desired length and then split into bolts

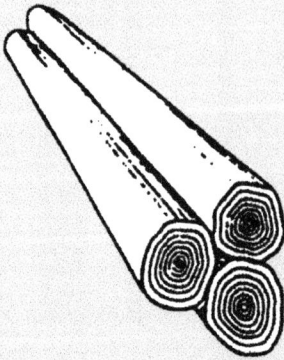

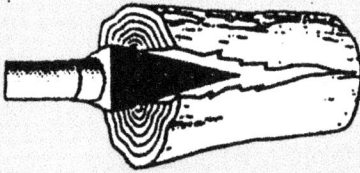

SPLITTING
The bolts are cut into stave wood

DRYING
The wood is dried outdoors and exposed to the weather for 3 years. It is sometimes kiln-dried after air drying.

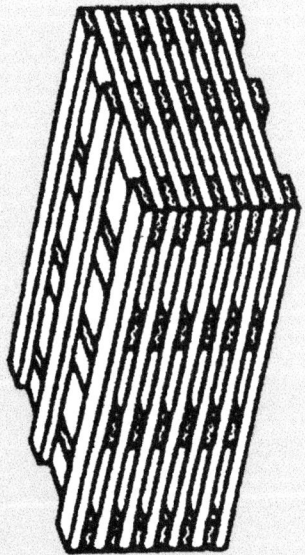

Planing and hollowing

Shaping and jointing

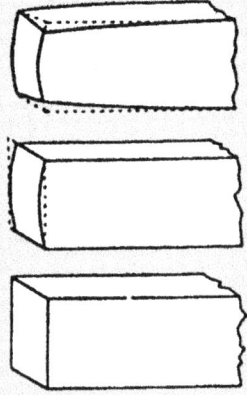

the staves are shaped…

RAISING THE BARREL AND BENDING
This is carried out with a windlass or bending machine

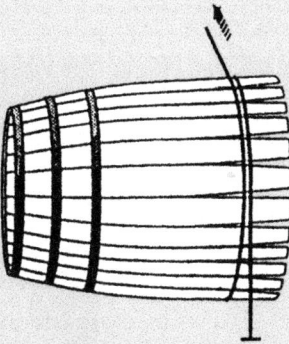

The wood is dampened outside and heated inside

The European technique:
Bending with a wood-fired brazier for about 20 minutes followed by futher heating.
5-10 min = light heating
10-15 min = medium heating
15-20 min = heavy heating

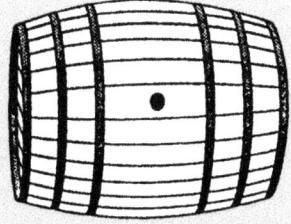

The American technique:
Steam bending followed by charring with a gas burner.
15 s = light char
30 s = medium char
45 s = heavy char

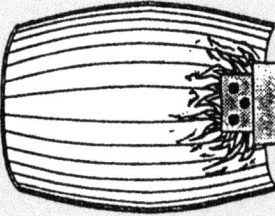

The final hoops are fitted and the barrel is tested with hot water.

MAKING THE HEAD PIECES
The heads are made up of 7-9 boards assembled with dowels. Strips of reed make the liquid tight.

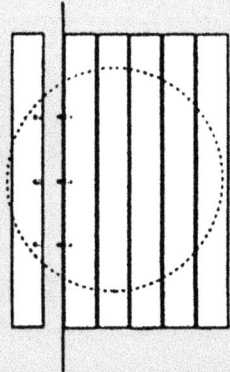

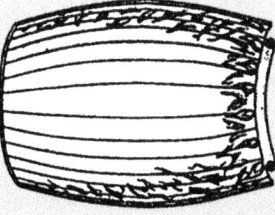

J.R. Mosedale and J.L. Puech, *Trends in Food Science & Technology*, 1998

[21]

Heating Process

With moisture sprayed in combination with the heat inside (from a brazier of chips), a windlass is used to progressively pull the staves together. Bending is a crucial step in barrel-making which, if not done properly, could result in leakage, cracks, splitting, and blisters. Blisters can be avoided by making small punctures inside the barrel staves.

Toastage

Temporary iron hoops are immediately installed to tighten the staves together. Before the heads are placed into the barrel, the barrel is then placed over a brazier, or an open wood fire fueled with oak chips, to receive its toastage. Depending on the aromatic profile demanded, the barrel-maker creates a specific toastage from very light to heavy, or char.

Toasting Type	Average Temperature (c)	Cycle 1* (min)	Cycle 2** (min)	Total Time
Traditional - Light	180°	35°	0°	35°
Traditional - Medium	200°	35°	1°	36°
Traditional - Medium +	220°	35°	3°	38°
Traditional - Medium ++	240°	35°	5°	40°
Long - Light	180°	60°	0°	60°
Long - Medium	200°	60°	0°	60°
Long - Medium +	220°	60°	0°	60°
Long - Medium ++	240°	60°	0°	60°
Intense	270°	0°	30°	30°

* Cycle 1: Low intensity heat. Slow and deep penetration. Tannins progressive thermal degradation.
** Cycle 2: Strong intensity heat. Light penetration. Aromas intensification and complexity.

Toasts

Depending on the origins and density of the oak, as well as the heat's duration and intensity, toastage offers a wide aromatic palate. This can range from fresh oak with notes of vanilla and coconut milk, progressing slowly to toasted bread, mocha, dark chocolate, then changing into coffee, chicory, and then to dark roasted beans. Finally the aromas turn to smoke, dried meat, and burnt spices. The cellar master, in coordination with the barrel-maker, designs the aroma profile to achieve the particular house character.

Techniques: Traditions and Innovations

Computer-modulated augers fueled by an oak toasting brazier allow the barrel- maker to have consistent and specific toasts. With this new device, and with the help of a fine mist of water in the barrel, you can obtain a "slow and deep" toast. This technique softens the tannins and allows the heat to penetrate deeper into the wood, an important step which gives the cellar master the ability to pinpoint and vary the barrel's flavor profile.

The methods of heating vary greatly in intensity, time, and technique between European coopers, ranging from a very light to a heavy toast. On the other side of the Atlantic, American cooperages are looking for a more intense and brief toastage to char the barrels for Bourbon and whiskey.

Although the traditional techniques have mostly been retained, research for more consistency and uniformity has opened doors to infrared and radio-frequency heating of the barrels.

Toast Profiles

Main Components

COMPONENTS	ODORS
Lactones: whiskey lactone	Coconut, fresh wood, underbrush
Aromatic Aldehydes	Vanilla
Phenols = the two main phenols are eugenol and guaiacol	Clove, carnations, smoke, toasted bread, spices, leather, sweat, spices, pharmaceutical odors, petroleum
Components from the heat—furfural	Toasted almonds, toasted bread, licorice, burnt sugar

European Oaks

La Chauffe Blanche (The White Toast Heat)
- 302° F (150° C) for 60 minutes, for a depth of 6 to 7 mm.
- Results: less smokiness, charcoal, and furfural characters.
- Brings freshness, minerality, and tension that gives a sensation in the mouth, and gives more length on the palate.

Light to Medium Toast for Limousin Oak
- 302 to 392° F (150 to 200° C).
- Large grain, fine structure, high tannic potentials.
- The heating lasts from 35 to 60 minutes, for a depth of 1 mm.
- Results: toasted vanilla, then spiciness.

Light to Medium Toast for Tronçais & Allier
- About 300° F—The temperature can vary greatly depending on the cooper.
- Fine grain, large structure, low tannic potential.
- Heating time is 60 minutes.
- Results: with finer tannins.

Heavy Toast
- 404° F (240° C); maximum 554° F (280° C), or the wood starts to catch on fire.
- Heating time is 35 minutes for a depth of +4 mm.
- Results: smoky and burnt with rich tannins.

American White Oak

This will have much lower tannins compared to the European varieties. In my experience, I think a heavy and long toast is preferable for spirits to soften the dill pickle character, leaving more space for the vanilla and the spices.

The Barrel

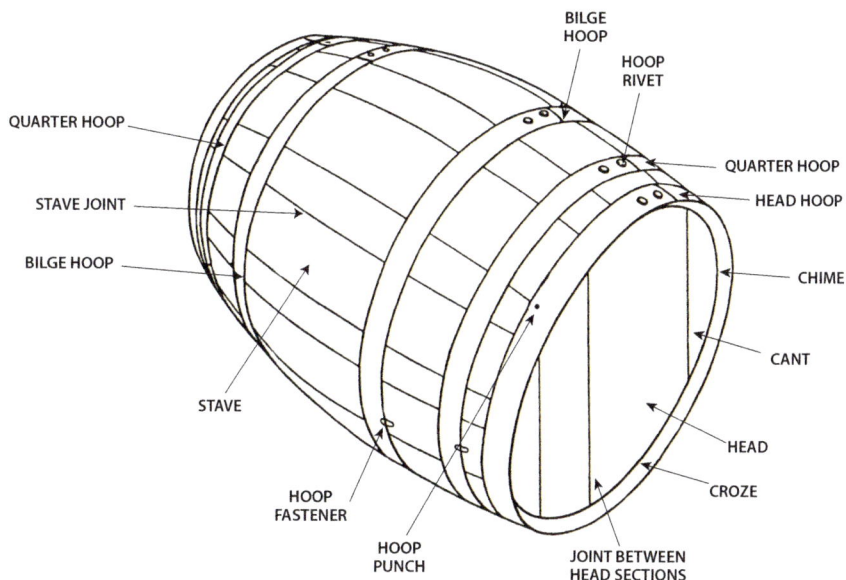

Courtesy: Barrel Builders, Inc.

Heads

The heads, which make up 25% of the inside surface of the barrels, are usually not toasted for spirits.

To ensure that the heads are liquid tight, the boards are assembled together with dowels and strips of reed inserted between them. Coopers never use metal for this purpose.

After grooves are made into both ends of the barrel and on the outside edge of the heads, the cooper puts the heads in place and seals them with a paste made of flour and water. (For gluten-free barrels, buckeye flour is used instead.)

Galvinized hoops replace the iron hoops to avoid rust, which is inevitable in high humidity. Before the use of iron, hoops were made from hazelnut or chestnut wood called whithies, which also made them easier to roll without soiling them. These hoops were stacked tightly together along the entire top and bottom third of the barrel.

Bungs

A bunghole is drilled into the center of the bilge. There are several types of bungs available for sealing a barrel:

- Oak, with a cotton cloth for gentle tightness. This will need a tool to open and close.
- Silicone, which must be resistant to higher alcohol or they will become soft and sticky, which is a sign of rapid degradation.
- Cork, with a parafined tissue (cloth). This is practical and quick to install or remove, and is also airtight. It is the best alternative so far for practicality and tightness.

Mix of Oak Staves

It is possible to order barrels made out of staves from different origins, grains, and with different toastages to gain complexity or to achieve a particular profile for a special blend.

Profile Inside a Barrel

In the last few years, various profiles, undulations, honeycombs, and small punctures have been offered to the cellar master to speed up and increase tannin extraction. In those cases, toastages are less consistent compared to a smooth surface, so it is important to be aware of the interplay of the variables time /tannins/alcohol/ surface area. Tannins can be more or less harsh, resulting in much more time required for the spirit to soften and digest them.

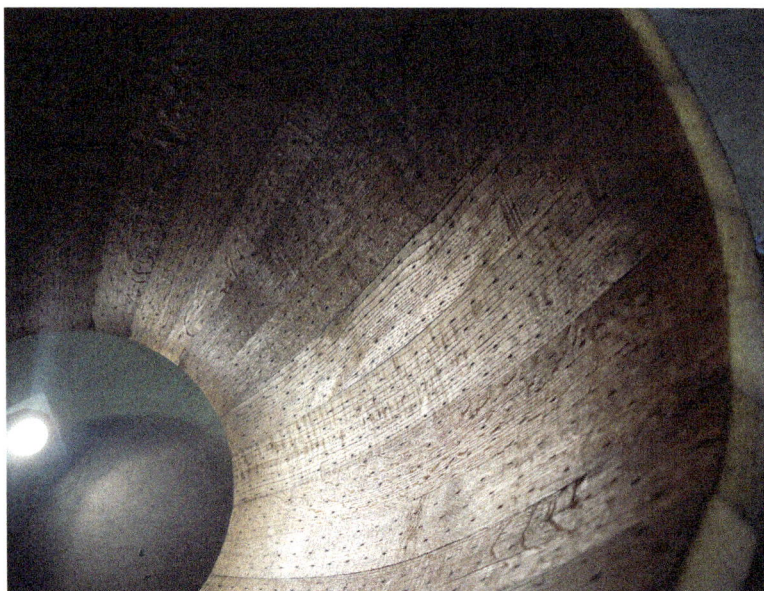

Courtesy: Tonnellerie Vicard

The Role of the Tannins

The tannins should have the role of a supporting cast but should not dominate the bouquet or they will upset the finesse, length, depth and balance of the spirit. The wood must be underneath: you guess it and you forget about it. Monitoring carefully the extraction of the tannins is one of the main tasks of the cellar master.

Kiln Drying

"*This mode of drying leads to physical degradation of the wood, resulting in a greater decrease of levels of lactones, volatile phenols, fatty acids, and norisoprenoids, especially when the humidity's range of the oak is elevated. The hot air destroys the enzymes of the wood so the different reactions don't occur, resulting in a strong bitterness and a lasting astringency. Consequently, the "steamed" oak doesn't offer a level of quality acceptable to the producer of premium spirits.*

—From "Journal of Cooperage Sciences and Techniques" (2000, vol. 6).

CHAPTER 4

Tannins and *Boisés*: Alternatives or Complements

Dried Tannins

Boisés, or oak-infused water, is not a substitute to obtaining traditional quality from new oak barrels, which is still by far the best way to age spirits. Rather, they are used to reinforce the structure, to adjust the amount of tannins and to enhance the mouth feel.

The shavings, beans, cubes, slabs, inserts, chips, and powder of oak wood are made from the same stave woods used for the construction of barrels. Oak wood tannins have been traditionally applied for many years for the production of all aged spirits such as brandy, Cognac, Armagnac, Calvados, rum, whiskey and Tequila. The advantage of these infusions is that they increase the concentration of the main volatile components by disintegrating the lignins (aromatic aldehydes) and vanillins.

The composition of oak tannins consists of about 45% cellulose, 22% hemicellulose, 25% lignin, and between 0.8 to 10% tannins, which are the pathway to an extreme complexity in spirits. To be released, these compounds need an open-air seasoning, a mechanical preparation (i.e., cutting the wood into the desired size and shape) and toasting. The tannins give color, take part in the flavors and taste, and make it possible for the spirits to evolve favorably during aging.

Toasting

Toasting temperature and total duration of the infusion are of the highest order, but another factor is the density of the wood. American oak is denser than French oak, and therefore the rate of heat penetration is quite different.; thus, the colors and flavors will be different. Research has shown that there is not a direct correlation between the flavor and the color.

Oak alternatives are toasted using a wide range of technology not employed by traditional cooperages. These products can be toasted for longer periods of time, and on all sides. This makes the overall impact of toasting more significant and results in an ever-increasing range of flavors.

Types Of Boisés

Based on the same method of extraction where only the ingredients differ due to the origin and the treatment, the results are aromatically very different. European oak, being more tannic, brings structure, richness (fat) and vanilla notes. American oak has a lighter structure, but is more aromatic with fruity notes of coconut, banana, pear and spicy accents.

Cellar masters need to use caution in using commercial oak extracts, which can be very heterogeneous. Because of the different methods of manufacture, the results could be far from original expectations.

The industrial process called thermo-treatment allows a uniform and consistent extraction, but modifies the aromatic characteristics caused by higher temperature (320–392° F) and time of infusion. With a temperature gradient at 320° F (160° C), the spicy notes are predominant. At 350° F (180° C), warm accents of vanilla, chocolate, and caramel come through, while at 392° F (200° C), coffee and torrefaction are more specific characters of an aged spirit.

By mixing, toasting to different levels and using oak from different origins, such as France, Eastern Europe, and America, new aromatic profiles are created that can be adapted to specific blends.

Making Boisés

After 5 years of use, barrels no longer have tannins to impart to a spirit. To compensate for this shortage, the cellar master has the option to adjust the blends with *boisés* to create the same consistency and organoleptic characteristics for the consumer.

All types of oak shavings are obtained during the construction of the barrels, vats, etc., meaning they have been air-dried outside for at least 3 years, not kiln-dried.

De-mineralized water is used such as rainwater, de-ionized water and distilled water. The use of any type of solvents is prohibited for taste and to keep the integrity of the products.

Extraction—The oak chips are infused for a period of 7 hours at a temperature between 203° F (95° C) to 210° F (99° C). To avoid a loss of the aromatic compounds, the liquid is always kept under the boiling point.

When the infusion time is over, the oak chips are withdrawn, and can be replaced by new ones for more concentration. The extraction is not made with alcohol due to the loss in evaporation.

Maceration—To cook with a gentle boiling—or better, a little below the boiling point—facilitates the reactions of hydrolysis, giving compounds with less bitterness and astringency. This process also facilitates the condensation and the precipitation of the tannins, forming a deposit at the bottom of the barrel or the tank, which will be removed by a gentle racking off.

Stabilization—Being an aqueous solution, the infusion has to quickly be stabilized with alcohol after decantation. The minimum level of fortification should be at least 25% abv or above. This operation should be made by very slowly adding the alcohol at 65% abv to the infusion; not the opposite, which burns the tannins and lowers the aromatic intensity.

Fortification—The quality and the type of the spirit being used for fortification, either for brandy, whiskey, rum, tequila, or others, is of primary concern.

Grape varietals, from more neutral ones as Ugni blanc, to the most aromatic as Riesling or Muscat, will create new entities, which will bring another level of complexity to your spirits. The proportion of lees and sediments left in the wine during distillation will also widen the structure by the contribution of the spicy fat.

It is quite beneficial for the tannins to have that coating during the aging process. The rancio character will come sooner due to a lower alcohol content, which improves the oxidation, resulting in more integrated tannins and a rounder mouth feel.

The same applies to apples and other fruits; sugar cane, grains, and roots. Making *boisés* earlier will give you flexibility, complexity, and consistency in the long run. In my experience with making *boisés*, you should start with the best ingredients available in order to achieve the quality you will be happy with in 5, 10 or 50 years. In very small quantities, they will bring you a special and precious tool for aging and blending.

Conservation and Regeneration of Barrels

Fortified *boisés* should also be used to keep empty barrels from drying out if they won't be filled in the next few weeks. Just put about 10 to 15 gallons in each barrel of 92 gallons (about 5 gallons in a 55-gallon barrel), then shake and turn them regularly. This way, you will not lose the alcohol absorbed by the wood, and will avoid the dismantling of the staves.

To regenerate old barrels, fill them completely with a much more concentrated *boisés* for the wood to soak the tannins through the fibers. By elevating the temperature, you will allow a deeper penetration inside the staves. In that case, leave some head space for the expansion of the liquid to avoid overflowing.

CHAPTER 5

Cognac Jules Robin & Cie

Aging or Maturation

The aging process obeys the cycle of life, and it is influenced by changes of season, the moon, the environment, and all natural and local conditions.

Whatever the type of spirit, the aging process will follow different periods of rest and oxidation during its life in the barrel. The nature of the ingredients, the type of yeast, the temperature of fermentation, the size and shape of the still, and single or double distillation will all shape the distillates.

After distillation, the young, clear, and fiery spirit will spend time in wood (essentially oak) to acquire different stages of maturity. During that period, which can last from a few years to decades, a transformation takes place, thanks to the genuine respiration happening through the wood revealed by the simultaneity of the absorption of oxygen and the rejection of carbonic gas.

We know that eaux de vie age faster when their alcohol content is lower. The extraction of the oak is optimal around 55% abv, but at this level the solubilization of the lignin is blocked, depriving the spirits of an important component. An influential factor of the extraction is temperature, which is optimal for aging between 75 and 85° F. The down side of it is an elevated level of evaporation and an increased percentage of volatile components detrimental to quality. The EDV becomes dried out with an odor of spoiled apple.

I have also noticed a disparity between Cognac and Armagnac and the New World brandies, due to the aromatic profiles of the grape varietals in conjunction with soil composition and microclimates.

After the first year of extraction, a relatively fast reduction of proof in a few steps over the course of years will allow the blend to marry longer. For a spirit intended to age three to five years—after the period of extraction—a reduction every few months will allow the water to be integrated with the alcohol. Consequentially, this is shortening the first phase—the oxidation of the tannins—when the EDV are chewy, mixed up and in flux. At that stage of aging, these EDV should be ignored until recovery.

For practical and qualitative reasons, it is important to have good organization of your inventory, with the young blends being more accessible in front and the old ones hidden in the best back corner of the cellar.

The Origin of Aromas

Aromas can have three different origins: (see the Aromas Chart in Appendix).

Primary Aromas—Their sources come from the original raw ingredients such as grapes, fruits, grains, sugar cane, roots and plants. Their quality will be predominant to the complexity and the harmony of the final product.

Secondary Aromas—The odors produced by the yeast during alcoholic fermentation, such as alcohol, aldehydes, esters, volatile acidity, and by malo-lactic fermentation, such as buttery or creamy aromas.

Tertiary Aromas—The extraction from the oak and the different periods of oxidation of the maturation process become more and more crucial for the formation of the bouquet.

In oak barrels, the primary aromas are progressively attenuated and one notices an important modification of the secondary aromas. The excess of volatile components diminishes and the less volatile ones will intensify.

These transformations will reveal past mistakes done either in the selection of the ingredients, during the fermentation, or in the course of the distillation process (i.e., decisions made about when to make the cuts or the speed and temperature of distillation).

Aging Periods

Three successive processes occur during the aging process:

Subtraction Function of Oak—After distilling in copper pot stills, the copper taste that was acquired during that time disappears after about 2 months.

Extraction of Oak Components—As a function of grape varietals, quality and the origin of the wood, size of the casks and the aging conditions, the duration of this period should be between 9 months to 1 year for a 92-gallon barrel, and a lot less for smaller barrels. The cellar master should be particularly vigilant not to over-extract tannins that will delay the next step and be detrimental to final quality.

Degradation: Hydrolysis—After the extraction period, the spirit should be transferred to neutral barrels. In the following years, some of the true characters will come back on the top of the oak; then, over 2 to 3 years, the spirit will go through a strong period of oxidation. The EDV develops a temporary and not very appealing chewy taste. The flavors are muddy and undistinguished (don't worry).

After the hydrolysis of the tannins takes place, the spirit recovers from these important transformations with aromas of sweet spices and vanilla, gaining more complexity and depth. It also acquires a warm amber color. At this stage of maturation, the spirit is appealing and ready to bottle.

Second Period of Oxidation

A second period of oxidation can be a path to a more completed maturity. Following the first oxidation, you have at least 5 years with a kind of stability. This phase of aging is continuous as long as the spirit is in an oak barrel, but follows some fluctuations and characteristics with the evolution of the components. The contribution of oxygen during pumping and the natural evaporation provide an acceleration of the oxidation. The *rancio* character comes from this evolution.

The dark amber color turns to brown, with a mahogany hue.

Rancio

The *rancid* character appears in spirits after many years of aging in wood, depending on the nature of the ingredients, the distillation process, type of wood, hygiene and temperature of the cellars, speed of reduction and, primarily, the proportion of fatty acids. The hydrolysis of the esters such as caprylate and ethyl laurate, releases the fatty acids whose oxidation creates ketones, offering a rich organoleptic character of dried leather, nuttiness, cedar, coconut, tobacco, and balsamic accents, produced by the different resins of the oak.

During this *maderization*, a chardonnay, a rye, a sugar cane spirit, or an agave spirit will develop the same profile, concentration, or range of flavors reminiscent of tawny ports, sherries with their nutty flavors, spices, and heady floral accents. The spirit shows mellower and deeper structure, offering an incredible length, which will persist for a long time in an empty glass.

The *rancio* contribution is fascinating, attractive, and quite powerful, but can also be overwhelming. At a certain level of concentration and intensity, it should be used with restraint in blends, like a rare and precious spice.

Is Rancio *a Goal in Itself?*

Yes— by providing depth, complexity, and viscosity to old spirits with the blossoming of tertiary aromas, both in the nose and on the palate.

No—blends can become oily, dried out, bitter, pungent and unbalanced if not aged or kept in ideal conditions.

CHAPTER 6

Cognac Guy Gautier & Cie

The Art of Blending

Cellar Master & Master Blender

Aging is inseparable from the art of blending. Depending on its elaboration and aging, every spirit has its own aromatic profile, which will be put to full use through its blending with other spirits that have different characteristics. This crucial and highly complex stage cannot be accomplished through the application of simple mechanical recipes. The master blender depends on empirical knowledge gained over the course of time and necessitating constant monitoring through tasting, along with a perfect sensory memory of aged spirits at their different stages of elaboration. Such knowledge, which requires many years of apprenticeship under the elders of the profession, has been differentiated, maintained, and transmitted through exchanges between master blenders, craft distillers, vine growers, merchants, brokers, and different governmental organizations, to raise and maintain the highest level of quality possible.

The Role of the Master Blender

"When it comes to assessing the interaction of hundreds of aroma compounds, the most sophisticated measurements tool remains the human nose." Rachel Barrie, master blender at Bowmore Whisky.

Due to their crucial role, master blenders of large companies, as in the perfume business, don't travel together as to avoid potential accidents, which could create a disastrous gap in continuity in the elaboration of their products.

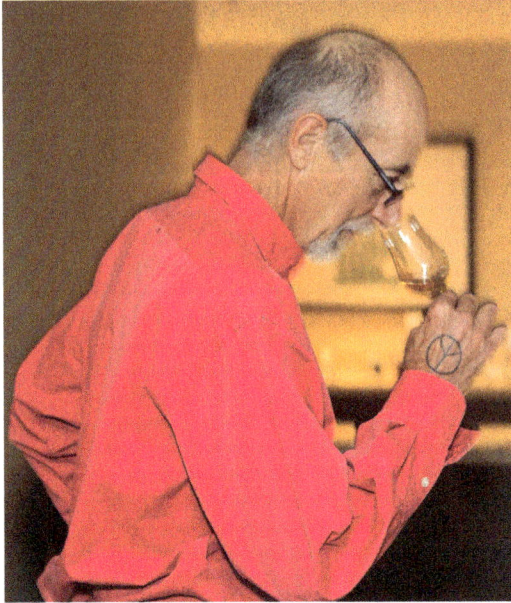

The author at work, photo © Andrew Faulkner

Qualities

The master blender must have a sense of vision with a good dose of common sense. The job requires determination, consistency, organization, passion, relentless patience, open mindedness, honesty, and integrity, plus a certain level of sophistication about food, wine, and spirits. This training should be done by a competent, informed, and experienced elder. He or she should have the ability to learn, listen, and taste with a lot of people of different origins, races, cultures, and sensibilities.

Role

The role of the cellar master/master blender is to use his or her long experience and intuition for making crucial and irreversible decisions by:

- Monitoring the aging process through decisions about what

type of oak barrels, their size, origin, toasting level, etc., and when to switch from new to old barrels and move the aging spirits from one cellar to another due to different aging conditions (i.e., dry or wet cellars).
- Scheduling the reduction of the blends over the years.
- Creating blends from different origins and ages.
- Tasting regularly to follow the evolution of the spirits over the years.
- Constantly controlling the aging process to maintain consistency in all levels of production.

The cellar master has to keep in mind that a succession of master blenders will oversee some of the aged spirits in the inventory, deciding their fates.

Blending: A Thirst for Quality

The aging process for spirits begins in the vineyards, the orchards, or the fields, where the ingredients are growing.

The cellar master/master blender should immerse himself in knowing the fields, vineyards, and topography of the area where the raw ingredients grow, in order to feel the places and their surroundings—to listen to "the speech of flowers and other voiceless things," in the words of French poet Charles Baudelaire. It is a never-ending story, a constant research to extract the essence from the crop destined for the final product. The thirst for quality requires vision, patience, consistency and abundant passion.

Blending is not a task in which one mixes different varietals from different ages and origins and then reduces the alcohol level with water... et voilà! It requires time for the different compounds to marry, to evolve and, consequently, to create new entities of flavors. It is an association of ideas that should entice and seduce.

To remain consistent over time, a producer should not put himself/herself into a dependent position beside vis-à-vis, a varietal, a vineyard or a grower. Keeping a certain flexibility with a base of three to four main sources of raw ingredients, plus small quantities of more marginal or aromatic varietals, will allow the master blender to carry out progressive changes. Sudden alterations from one blend to another under the same label and quality are not perceived favorably by consumers.

The way to proceed when creating a blend is to envision it before making it. Then, following your previous yearly notes and evaluations, you select the spirits that will be the structure and the body of your blend.

We call them coupe-mère, or mother-blend, or skeleton structure: They will constitute 80% of your final blend. The ideal approach is to make different ones from slender to heavy that you will be assembling proportionately in order to reach balance. You always will look for a fine-tuning by according the different varietals and the age of the spirits.

After months of marriage, new aromas emerge which can surprise you. The association of different profiles give birth to completely new entities that are not part of the original blends. Consequently, a cautious approach is wisely recommended when blending.

The pyramidal construction of a blend is similar to the elaboration of perfumes with notes from the heaviest and most persistent components that form the structure as a trail and a fixateur. Then, the body or heart, in the middle, determines the theme of the blend, and they usually have a medium volatility. At the top of the pyramid, the head notes, which are the most volatile and fleeting, bring accents and complexity.

Because of the variability of the ingredients of the distillation and of the aging process, proportions don't follow rigorous physical parameters. Nevertheless, the lower base components could represent about 20–30%, the body 60–70%, and the top 5–10%.

Having diversity in your inventory will give more flexibility and more options into the construction of blends, and will also allow you to reserve some particular barrels for single barrel, single vintage or single varietal. To maintain consistency, I always create at least 30% more of the blend than I need for my next bottling, and will then use what remains in the following one as a base for continuity and for a better integration in the next blend.

The ultimate accomplishment for a master blender is to create the perfect assemblage from a bouquet of olfactory impressions, representing and called "the peacock tail"[1]— a symbol of diversity, beauty, and power. The term peacock tail is used for brown spirits when they display the spectrum of nuances, complexity, balance and perfection that you can only find at the peak of their maturity.

1   The flamboyant plumage is used in a courtship ritual, called lekking, which can last for days. This is an example of patience and determination.

[45]

CHAPTER 7

Inventory

Performing yearly evaluations of the inventory is crucial during the aging process in order to determine the fate of the spirits. The cellar master decides either to blend, to release as a single barrel from a single vineyard or single varietal, or keep it longer to reach complete maturity.

The tasting of inventory needs to be done blind, and the use of blue tasting glasses is recommended to avoid being influenced by the identity of the samples and their colors. Of course, you should not look at your tasting notes from previous years before current evaluation.

In case a sample puzzles you due to a defect, oxidation, or other reasons, another sample needs to be taken first from the same barrel and then from other similar ones for comparison.

Taking Samples

To avoid mistakes, it is desirable to have two people involved in this operation, which necessitates a strict accuracy. This way, both people can check the samples to ensure the label, barrel number, and percentage of alcohol by volume are all correct.

Before you begin tasting, have all the sample bottles prepared in their boxes with proper labels. Brown bottles ought to be used to protect the liquid from the light.

Mix the barrel thoroughly before taking a sample to unify the liquid. The tannins tend to stay on the side and at the bottom of the new barrels, which can mislead your results and give you an inaccurate evaluation.

After rinsing the bottles with the barrel's contents, take two samples: One will be for history (we are mortal, after all!), and the other for comparative tastings.

Record and classify all your samples in a logbook with all necessary information. Labels should have the DSP number, lot number, date, barrel number, alcohol content, and description (varietal, vintage, yeast, origin, oak origin, and toastage). For optimum conservation and security, the sample bottles should be kept and locked in a dark, cool, dry place.

I always take samples for evaluation when the spirits are dormant (February) and start tasting them for complete evaluation from April to July.

Conservation in the Bottles

After bottling, spirits do not age in glass, yet become softer, rounder, and more harmonious. They acquire another dimension of fullness, even if oxidation has stopped. Bottles should be kept properly— standing in a dark and cool place—not near a radiator, fireplace, in the light or under the sun.

Partial Bottles

According to connoisseur Daniel Hallee from the Oenothèque in Paris:

"A bottle three-quarters full retains at least a year; a mid-level, six months. Passed this cap, the spirit loses its aromatic qualities very quickly; it oxidizes and takes even a slight ascessence. When a bottle is filled less than a quarter, it is better to finish it in three to four months."

Spirits that are aged naturally (without addition of water to lower the degree of alcohol) have greater longevity; manipulation always makes them more fragile.

To avoid deterioration of the precious libations of your liquor cabinet, you can:

- Adjust the level to be full with glass marbles. This is a good way to keep track of your drinking habit, or that of others.

- Pour the liquid in smaller bottles so the liquid fills up the bottle.
- Use a nitrogen canister to fill the headspace—the empty space above the liquid.

CHAPTER 8

Cellar at Cognac Braastad

Cellars

The aging process of spirits involves controlled evaporation, resulting in a concentration of flavors, a lessening of the volume and changes in percentage of alcohol.

Cellar Atmosphere

A humid atmosphere will result in a slow evaporation, causing a decrease in the strength of the alcohol. The spirit thus becomes softer and rounder.

A dry cellar will result in more water evaporation and a reduction of the volume, with an increase in the alcohol concentration. The spirit is harsher, shorter and more aggressive. There will also be a stronger extraction of the tannins, resulting in a burnt smell.

The difference in taste, whether sweeter and harsher, or delicate and floral with more finesse, will often appeal differently to consumers throughout the world. For example, the Asian market appreciates a stronger character, with more tannins and caramel, which is capable of resisting dilution by the addition of ice cubes and soda.

Cellar Construction

The ideal cellars in which to produce harmonious and balanced spirits are built with: a dirt floor; insulated low ceiling to reduce air space; doors and windows tightly closed to avoid drafts—all resulting in a loss of humidity, which is detrimental to the quality and is uneconomical, due to increased evaporation. In the case of dry cellars with concrete floors, the cellar should be equipped with temperature and humidity control.

It is important to make sure your distillery and the storage areas don't have chemicals, odors of any type, or off-aromas that would be detrimental to your spirits. Higher alcohol is more susceptible to absorbing aromas; thus, it is a good idea to refuse visitors wearing perfumes, and ban cooking or microwaving in the production areas.

Humidity

The optimum conditions of aging are with a humidity range between 75 to 85%. When the atmosphere is too dry, such as 50% or below, the spirits become harsher, more aggressive and leaner. If the cellar is too humid (+95%), the spirit looses body and structure, becoming what is known as flabby.

Temperature

It is good to allow a range different temperatures during the year in order for the alcohol to contract and to expand inside the barrel. This natural rhythm makes the spirit work and evolve better during spring, summer, and fall. The desirable range of temperature desirable falls between 50° F (10° C) and 75° F (25° C). It can be colder, but the distillate becomes dormant and the extraction is minimalized. On the other hand, anything above 75° F (25° C) causes the evaporation to dramatically increase, resulting in a consequent financial loss.

In a perfect cellar, a spirit stored in a 92-gallon oak barrel at 70% abv will naturally reach 40% abv after 45 to 50 years, without the addition of water.

Humidification

To control the level of humidity, a humidifier is the easiest and most consistent solution. Otherwise, spraying the concrete and the top of the barrels (taking care not to spray the sides where you have written the barrels' information) will help in providing humidification. The next day, be sure to push back the puddles of water in order to avoid having your spirits take on the smell of stagnant water.

CHAPTER 9

Courtesy: American Distilling Institute

Barrels: Preparation, Maintenance, and Repairs

Inspecting

Outside—After removing the plastic and cardboard wrapping, look for any damage that has been caused during transportation and handling.

- Barrels should be smooth and well sanded.
- There should be no gaps between staves.
- There should be no signs of cracked staves, particularly in the bilge area.
- The cracking of staves, especially at the bilge, is often a sign that the wood was not heated sufficiently or properly prior to bending. The staves are heated during the shaping process and water is applied inside the barrel. Moisture soaks into the wood, giving it some flexibility. Cracked staves are most common in the staves with the bunghole.
- Hoops should be evenly spaced on the barrel and hoop nails driven in properly.
- Hoop rivets are aligned on the same stave.
- Galvanizing is uniform, meaning no flakes or chips.
- Head hoops are flush with—or extend—just a bit above the top of the chime.

- No noticeable bowing in the heads.
- The bunghole is smooth, tapered and cauterized.

Inside—With a small flashlight, inspect the inside of the barrel.
- Smell the barrel. A good barrel should smell like lightly toasted oak.
- A bad barrel smells like mold or wet earth.
- Kiln dried oak smells like dill or green wood.
- Barrels used previously for wine, cider and other products weak in alcohol can develop an aldehyde-like smell that resembles nail polish or vinegar.
- The toast level should be even and uniform, with no charring or blisters.
- Look for sawdust; it can be confused with a certain type of mold.
- Mold can grow inside a wine or cider barrel, but not in a spirit barrel, except if the previous liquid was under 20% abv.
- An alcohol solution of 25% abv will kill the mold over a few days (don't use this in blends).
- Treatment with sulfur is a no-no for spirits, for obvious reasons: It gives a burning sensation in the nose and palate, which is impossible to eliminate.

Installing the Barrels

Place the barrels on 4"×4" timbers to be able to roll and shake them easily. First, rinse the barrel with a few gallons of hot water to remove sawdust. Then fill the barrels completely with hot water (I use the hot water from the condenser of the pot still, which is the perfect temperature of 180° F). Steam is too hot and kills the enzymes of the wood, causing aromatic loss.

Tightly insert the bung in the barrels and let it soak overnight. The advantage of this method versus testing them with air pressure is that you remove the first bitter tannins on the inside of the barrels or vats.

The next morning, carefully inspect the barrels for leaks. Be careful of the vacuum pressure when you remove the bung. If you purchase from a quality barrel-maker, you should not have any leaks. Empty the barrels and rinse them a few more times with clean, cold water. Keep them upside down for a few hours to drain them entirely. If you don't plan to fill them in the next 2 days, cover the bungholes with a thin cloth to avoid insects, especially fruit flies.

At this point, the barrels are ready to receive your precious spirit. You can fill them with just distilled spirit for aging or, if you don't use them soon, you can prepare a solution at 30% abv to be used over and over again. Put a few gallons in the barrels, then roll and shake them regularly until you fill them.

Bungs

Traditionally, wooden bungs are used for spirits and are held in place with a piece of cloth. They need to be punched down with a special tool to make a tight seal, resulting most of the time in cracks near the bunghole. They are made of redwood, fur or oak.

For practical reasons, corked bungs with a parafined cloth are very convenient. You can install or remove them with one hand. They are fairly tight and sit level with the staves.

Silicon bungs—I have tried different ones over the years. Most of them don't resist the attack of alcohol, and become either soft and sticky, or hard and discolored. Being unsure about their neutrality, I stopped using them.

Coating or Painting

Both are detrimental to the breathing through the wood, plus they are unnecessary to prevent insect borers. Unlike for wine, borers are quick to come back when they smell the strong alcohol in the wood. So far, I have never had a leak.

Racks

Wooden racks that are most secure against earthquakes are reinforced with metal cross-cables and bars and anchored into the floor. Because they are fixed securely in place, they provide greater security while pumping in and out from the barrels. With proper dimension, it saves time and reduces handling. Having three rows of barrels on both sides, you are able to fill more efficiently and write and record on the barrel and cards for better organization.

CHAPTER 10

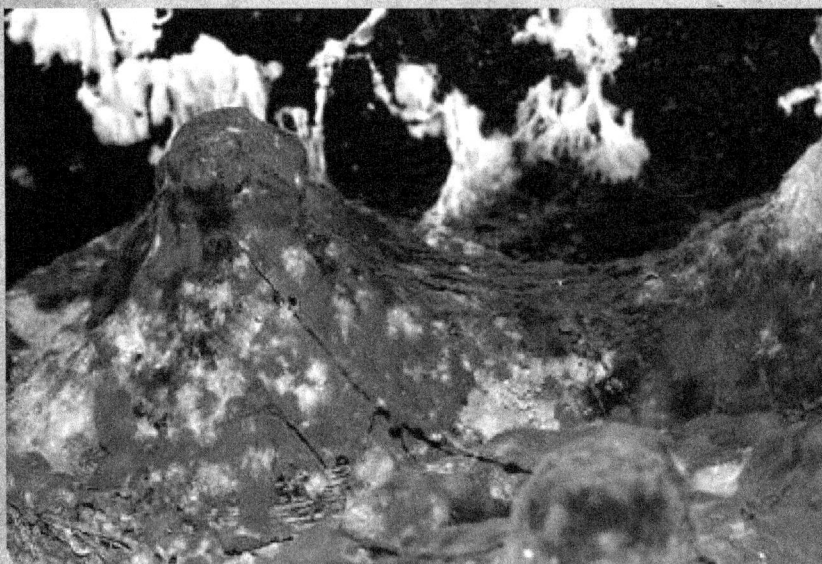

The mold *Torula compniacensis*, found on the walls, ceilings and roofs of old cognac aging cellars; photo courtesy Jesse Nash and Barney Lehrer

Torula

In cellars filled with barrels of spirits, there are a few types of microscopic fungi that develop, which can cover and blacken walls and ceilings. They grow especially well in cellars where the oldest and best spirits are aging. In 1881, Dr. Richar, a well-known mycologist, identified and classified this particular black fungus as a *Torula compniacensis*.

Another fungus, Cradosporium, grows only inside on the walls and on the barrels and is used as a support for the Torula. These other species are white, green, red, brown, or black. These fungi are nourished by the alcoholic vapors and flourish in a cool, dark, damp environment.

The fungi's roles are quite important in the aging process because their enzymes break down cellulose and lignin molecules of oak barrels they are covering. They have pronounced, persistent odors of aged spirit such as leather, balsamic, cedar and nutty accents.

This microflora is fundamental to the development of the rancio flavor.

CHAPTER 11

Photos this page and facing page, courtesy: Camper English/alcademics.com

The Paradise

The light is dim and the stagnant atmosphere penetrates you with its cold and tense air, chilling your bones. You feel the stillness of time. You walk cautiously because of the low ceiling and spider webs. The odors of old spirits and fungus surround you, permeating senses deep in your body and soul.

In the gloaming, you discover the hidden treasures full of mysteries in the foggy immobility of this cavern: You are in Paradise.

There, demijohns line the dark shelves and very old barrels of different sizes—from 10 gallons to tierçons (132 gallons)—sit, preserving history, waiting faithfully for future generations.

CHAPTER 12

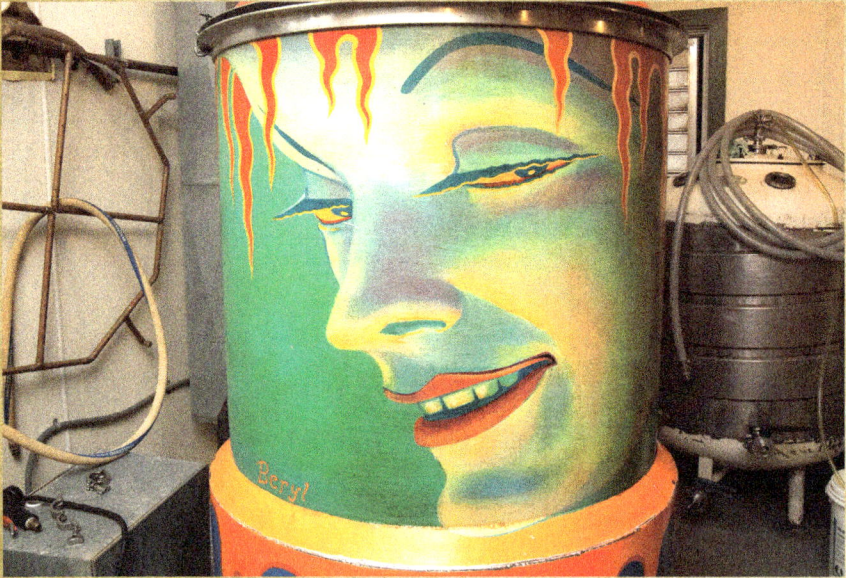

Painted tank at Cornelius Pass Distillery in Oregon; photo © Andrew Faulkner

Cellar Work

Careful attention to detail in the cellar will make a big difference in the quality of your spirits. Below are some rules that will help to ensure the quality of the spirits in your cellar:

- Don't use plastic tanks, hoses and fittings, because they are not resistant to chemicals. Stainless steel (316) is good for to use, as is brass or copper.
- Be aware that 304 stainless steel tanks will impart a metallic taste if you store spirits in them, and it does not take long at all for this to happen.
- NEVER use barrels that previously contained heads, tails, *secondes* or *brouillis* for spirits. They will taint your *eau de vie* forever.
- Be sure to empty hoses and pumps after each use, rinse them and let them drain completely. You will be disappointed when off-odors develop and deposit persistent smells in the *eau de vie*.
- Do not cross contaminate by using the same hoses and tools for your EDV as for the distillation fractions (heads, brouillis, and tails) or for wine, cider, wash, etc.
- Keep doors closed to avoid draft and sunlight in the barrel's storage, as this increases evaporation and lowers humidity.
- Turn off lights in the area when you are not working. Lights produce heat, absorb humidity and disturb the tranquility

of the spirits; plus, you save energy.

- Be organized, as it promotes the efficiency of everybody involved, and it helps to avoid mistakes and reduces stress.

When filling the barrels with spirits, leave head space to allow for expansion due to the elevation of temperature in your cellar. It is called the "Rule of Thumb"—The tip of your thumb should touch the liquid as you reach through the bunghole. If you can feel the top of the fill level of the liquid, you have reached a good level.

CHAPTER 13

Solera System

The Solera technique is a trickle-down system of aging that is used mainly in Spain and regions that were at one time under Spanish rule. Producers of Sherry, Madeira, brandy, rum, wine, and even vinegar have been using it for centuries.

Barrels are stacked in horizontal and vertical rows with the oldest liquid stored at the bottom, which is then partly withdrawn for bottling. The barrels are then refilled with younger spirit from the row above. This system allows great consistency in the blending, but it tremendously reduces the creativity of the master blender, the specificity of the ingredients, and the richness of diversification.

CHAPTER 14

Evaporation

During aging in oak barrels (based on 92-gallon barrel capacity), and depending on temperature, humidity levels, storage height of barrels, and percentage of alcohol, a natural evaporation through the wood occurs on an average of 2–3.5% annually.

In warmer regions, evaporation can exceed 10% (based on 55-gallon-barrel capacity) for U.S. production of rum, cachaça, mezcal, tequila, and also bourbon and whiskey.

In high humidity conditions, more alcohol will evaporate than water, rapidly reducing the alcohol strength of the distillates. On the opposite end, under very dry conditions, more water evaporates, resulting in an increase of alcohol content.

Evaporation increases dramatically in proportion to the size of barrels. The smaller the barrels, the more evaporation occurs, with an increase in tannin extraction.

In big vats of 2,000 gallons or more, evaporation slows to 1.2%, but the aging is also much slower.

This natural and desirable evaporation has different names, depending on the regions and or countries in which spirits are produced. The most common name is "Angels' Share," but you will also find names such as "Angels' Tribute," "Angels' Portion" (Spain), and the "Angels' Tax" (South America).

Another name representing the different perceptions and regional culture is the "Devil's Share" in the Calvados region of France. The moral of this story is that the angels and devils are sharing and drinking at the same speakeasy. Perhaps for the barrels traveling on ships or stored under the water by kinetic aging (i.e., produced by the energy of a mass in movement), the appropriate name should be the "Mermaids' Share"!

In the 1970s, an experiment was conducted in Cognac, in which barrels were covered with plastic to study the evaporation's difference over one year. Although a few tenths of a percent of alcohol were saved, the aging process, in terms of oxidation and mellowness, slowed down dramatically. The level of extraction from the barrels remained roughly the same. I called it the "Angels Diet."

In all cases, it is important to keep the angels (or the devils) happy. Too little evaporation makes them sad and grumpy, but too much makes them drunk and inattentive, spending their time dancing on the barrels.

CHAPTER 15

Reduction and Water

The reduction of alcohol from cask to bottling strength should always be done slowly, with the water and the spirit at the same temperature. Because of the hundreds of components in the alcohol, the *assemblage*—or blend—needs time to absorb the water and to be married. This discipline from the master blenders illustrates a commitment to quality, consistency and the seriousness to all stages of production.

It is extremely important to never reduce the EDV bluntly or quickly. For example, when the alcohol content of the spirit is 70% abv or greater, you should not bring it down to 40% abv at one time, even if you are using pure water. This causes hydrolysis of the esters, resulting in a *saponification* of the spirit. In other words, it will taste like soap. The EDV becomes cloudy. This effect is exaggerated with spirits distilled on the lees, in which case you will notice a blue haze. After such a shock, the spirit becomes flat and has lost a good portion of its complexity and balance. It will never completely recover from this violent transmutation.

You can make the final reduction from 41.5 to 40% abv using spirits that are already cut to no less than 20% abv—already aged for at least the same time as the youngest EDV in your blend. This method allows a faster integration but requires more storage vessels, like neutral vats or casks.

Depending on the aging conditions of your cellar and the size of the barrels, a spirit just distilled will need about 45 to 50 years for the alcohol to drop from 70 to 40% abv without the addition of pure water. The volume will drop from 92.5 gallons at 70% abv to 26 gallons at 40% abv.

During the aging period, the cellar master reduces his or her EDV step by step, or blends to prepare them gradually for bottling.

A lot of water is necessary to monitor these slow but punctual operations. The importance of the water's quality and origin are of primary concern to achieve the level of quality you want to achieve.

The choices of water available are:
- Distilled water—neutral, dry, dead, with no volume
- De-ionized water—neutral, with a little more volume
- Spring or well water—the mineral sediments will over time settle down in the bottles even with tight and cold filtration. It usually happens under 55% abv.
- Rainwater—round, sweet, soft, with volume and a nice flesh. This is the best choice by far. I experimented and created the same blend, one reduced with distilled water and the other with rainwater. The result was like night and day in terms of quality, fullness, and mouth feel.

Before using water from the sky, the cellar master has to send samples of water to a lab for traces of pollution. Purity will differ depending on your geographic location, time of year, direction of the wind, and level of industrialization in your area. It is important to address these problems earlier rather than later to avoid potential lawsuits due to allergies or physical reactions by the consumer.

How to Process and Collect Rainwater

At the beginning of the rainy season, clean the roof of your distillery or cellar thoroughly of debris, dust and leaves, especially in the gutters and drains. Let the rain rinse the rooftop for a few hours.

Collect the rain in a tank. Filter it immediately with a household water filter and store it in a plastic or stainless steel tank in a dark and cool place. You will be able to use it for a few weeks.

Each time before using it, you should inspect and taste it: 1) Visually—check it by very slowly pouring the water. If it starts to become a bit oily, either re-filter it or discard it. 2) Smell and taste—look for a moldy or stagnant smell.

Take a sample in a glass and agitate it, then let it rest for a few minutes. Then re-smell and re-taste it. Usually, odors from the tank dissipate with aeration.

CHAPTER 16

Esoteric Natural Aging

Kinetic Aging

These experiments are entirely natural. There is no manipulation or addition to the spirit. Temperature change, humidity, pressure, climatic conditions, plus movement, accelerate the aging process, but also increase the natural evaporation that I call the "Mermaid's Share." This process is a *kinetic maturation* defined as *aging by the energy of a body in motion.*

Seven Fathoms Rums in the Cayman Islands

The process calls for a two-step maturation: One takes place above the water to allow for reductive oxidation of the spirit; the other takes place underwater for the benefit of kinetics. Barrels are sealed, using a patented process and chained to the ocean floor at a depth of seven fathoms (42 feet). In addition to the rocking and rolling motion provided by currents and waves, the rum undergoes another unique phase. Due to the pressure differential provided by the tidal change, the spirit moves back and forth through the wood of the staves, resulting in an acceleration of the aging process. I have not had the opportunity to compare samples at different stages of this process.

Fram: The Monster Ship of Norwegian Steel

Named for an ancient king of Norway, the *Fram* left from the Port of the Moon in Bordeaux, France, on March 30th, 2011, with 164 Scandinavian tourists aboard and a barrel of XO Cognac, made by Cognac Braastad. The 376-foot-long and 66.5-foot-wide boat traveled at a speed of 16 knots, carrying 318 passengers and crew.

The Cognac: XO Superior, with a minimum age of 12 years and an average age of 25 years, was a blend of Grand Champagne, Petite Champagne, Borderies, and Fins Bois—the 4 best appellations of the region. The reduction of the alcohol contents had been made with ice water from 1) the Antartic—S 72° 01' E 002° 46', and 2) Artic—N 69° 45.6' W 050° 22.44'. The 350 liter (92 gallon) barrel was filled with spirit at 41.6% abv. and sealed with a sworn oath from Mr. Fallon of the Bureau National du Cognac.

The boat first headed north to Oslo, Norway, and then to Greenland for the summer. Then, in September, it headed in the direction of New York. For this part of the trip, the barrel was stowed on the upper deck in its sealed golden cage. By demand of U.S. custom officials, the barrel had to be moved to the hold. In October, the *Fram* traveled to Usuiha in Argentina, then past the Cape Horn, navigated near the South Pole, before returning to the Bay of Biscay in Bordeaux, in April 2012—more than one year after leaving.

The return of the Fram with Richard Braastad; photo courtesy Fabien Cottereau

Cellar Master Richard Braastad was there to welcome back his baby and transported the cask back to Jarnac (12 km from Cognac) to be unsealed, tasted and compared with its twin barrel that had been left in the cellar.

After one year of rolling and reeling on the oceans and subjected to the influences of different maritime conditions of temperature and humidity, the precious liquid went through obvious changes… for the better!

Upon return, the barrel contained 305 liters (80.5 gallons) at 40.7% abv. An evaporation of 14.7% had occurred—more than four times the rate of that under normal cellar conditions. Enough Cognac remained to fill only 405 bottles.

Tasting notes from Cellar Masters Richard Braastad and Hubert Germain-Robin

- Before—Dried fruits forward, light attack, medium length, spices and oak tannins not fully integrated; light almond *rancio* character in the second part.

- After—More polished, gentle rising sensations; more mature, with a deeper, fatter *rancio* and an old leather character. The finish was elegant, firm and long. The harmony between the different components had greatly improved, especially the spices. During our tasting, we estimated the maturation gain from the one-year journey to be the equivalent of five years.

Pyramid-Aging

The great pyramid of Cheops in Egypt was built 5,000 to 10,000 years ago. There is still a debate among Egyptologists, archaeologists, scientists, mathematicians, astronomers, and researchers about its age.

The pyramid measures 492 feet (150 meters) in height, has a base surface of 13.6 acres and weighs about 13.2 million pounds. The prolonged diagonals of the monument are at the equilibrium point of the continents, which have equal repartitions on each side of the meridians. Each face of the great pyramid is facing a cardinal point. All those facts, and many more, are deeply mysterious and are not due to good fortune, coincidence, or chance.

Many experiments have been made in pyramids of different proportions. For example, instead of rotting when placed inside the pyramid, meat, fish and fruits were dehydrated and tasted delicious.

Bergeron: Glass pyramid to age wine

Vjictor Bergeron, an American of French origin, has aged bottles of wine, placed on the side with the neck oriented towards the north. Instead of stopping or slowing the evolution, as in the previous experiences, pyramids accelerate the maturation of the wine. In a few weeks, one obtains an aging of a few years. A comparative tasting was made in Bordeaux, with the participation of expert wine brokers who certified an undeniable difference.

Based on those facts and experiences, Master Distiller Jean-Paul Margot and I, in 1979, built a pyramid with proportional measurement (1/200) to age a small barrel (1 L) of VSOP Cognac in the location of the Pharoah's chamber. (In the real pyramid, this is situated in the middle, at about 138 feet above ground level.)

Made out of rigid cardboard, we oriented our monument along a north–south axis. After waiting three long weeks, we opened the pyramid, extracted the barrel and compared the Cognac to a control sample.

Tasting notes from the experiment:

- Tannins in the pyramid-aged barrel were definitely softer and melted in the blend.
- The oxidation period had been accelerated to reach another level of maturity.
- Spices became predominant, meaning a progression of tertiary aromas.
- Tasting notes from Mr. Paul Giraud, Master Distiller/ Master Blender at Boutiers, near Cognac: *In comparing both samples, the Cognac became a little drier, dustier and leathery, with traces of rancio (characters found in older spirits).*

CHAPTER 17

Finishing Spirits
in Used Barrels

Whiskey[1]

Spirits finished in European oak (*Quercus robur*) take on characteristics of sherry, dried fruit, raisins, candy peel, spices, cinnamon, nutmeg, wood, caramel, orange and English Christmas pudding.

The standard American oak (*Quercus alba*) barrel (known as ASB, 52.8 gallons/200 liters) is considered to mature whiskey at the optimum rate because of the ratio between the surface area of the cask and volume of spirit contained. American oak bourbon barrels are currently used by 90% of whiskey producers in the world, and contribute flavors of vanilla, honey, coconut, almonds, hazelnuts, butterscotch, fudge, spices, and ginger.

Rum

Most rum is matured in used bourbon or other whiskey barrels to impart some degree of seasoning. Many distilleries are currently finishing rums in sherry casks of Spanish oak, Madeira casks of American oak, and brandy barrels of French oak to add complexity and bring different distinctive personalities to their line of products.

Due to the climate, temperature and humidity of the Caribbean, the rate of maturation is about three times faster than in the Northern hemisphere, but comes at the cost of evaporation at more than 12%.

---

[1]　From *Whiskey for Everyone* (http://www.whiskyforeveryone.com/)

CHAPTER 18

Traditional Methods of *Élevage*: Syrup and Caramel

For centuries, the spirits industry allowed three different products to be added to spirits of quality: syrup, caramel, and *boisé*. Although some producers avoid them due to their style or philosophy, they bring tools to the cellar master to achieve softness, consistency, coloration and an appealing balance to their products, especially the younger ones or for the Asian markets, which appreciate spirits with more oak, color, and sweetness. But if your goals are purity, dryness, and more focused rising sensations, then these tools are not for you. In that case, the quality of the wood (the natural pentoses of the oak) provides aromatic richness and good balance.

Syrup

Obscuration from the syrup affects measurement of the degrees of alcohol in the spirit. It is rare to have more than 2% sugar in solution; equivalent to about 8 grams per liter. Early addition, many months before bottling, is necessary for good integration into the blend.

A syrup is a sugar concentrate aqueous solution, and the best are made from pure sugar cane. Fruits like cherries, strawberries, raspberries, red and black currants, blackberries and pomegranates make fruits syrup very appealing and useful for liqueurs and confectionary. Other compound syrups are enriched with more aromatic ingredients such as lemon, lime, orange, or medicinal plants, roots and herbs—by decoction or infusion. Examples of syrups from the lightest in color and density to the darkest caramel are jelly, thread, softball, hardball, small crack, crack, hard crack and caramel.

Cooking and Preparation

Syrups can be made cold with equal parts sugar and distilled water, but those prepared hot preserves better. However a certain point of balance is crucial: a syrup that is not cooked enough ferments and spoils; but when a syrup is overcooked, the sugar crystallizes at the bottom of the bottle.

Use an open copper pot with double wall and steam injection. It is possible to use direct fire, but be careful with the danger of rimage (burn) due to the intensity of direct fire or the concentration of heat at one place. Always use a long wooden paddle for mixing.

Preparation

- Charge the pot with 10.5 gallons (40 liters) of distilled water, 130 lbs (60 kilograms) of pure granulated sugar cane in large grains.
- Steam: 3 kilos/bars of pressure.
- Boiling point: 3 minutes, 15 seconds.
- Remove from the fire and pour into a copper or stainless steel container through a sleeve of flannel to filter the deposit.
- Yields 19 gallons (72 liters) of brut syrup (known as soufflé) at a density of 1,320 grams per liter.

The next day, when the syrup is lukewarm, add alcohol: one part brut syrup with two parts EDV at 50% abv, resulting in syrup/EDV mix at approximately 33% abv with a density of 1,062 grams per liter. This fortification prevents fermentation and molding during aging. Filtration should occur just after the addition of the EDV, so the blend is homogeneous. Paper filters, fabric of white wool, flannelette, canvas, and silk can be used after being rinsed with clean water.

Aging of Fortified Syrup

Always use the best ingredients (pure sugar cane) to obtain the best quality in your spirits.

In order to match with your legal declaration of age, the EDV used for fortification of the syrup should be at least the same age as the minimum age of your blend. Keep the syrup at least one year in an old barrel for resting and aging before use. Fortified syrups should be aged for more than 15 years before being added to old blends, such as XO.

After storing, rack off the syrup very slowly to leave any sediment at the bottom of the barrel.

Caramel for Color

Caramel is used in very small quantities to obtain consistency of color in your blends. Whereas wood tannins fade a little over time, caramel reinforces and fixes the color. The consumer expects to have the same hue for the same product with the same label year after year. Some parts of the world like to have their spirits with more coloration. You could obtain a deep color from new oak, but the spirit will have an unpalatable and bitter taste.

Make caramel using a double-wall copper kettle, same as for syrups.

Preparation:

- Charge the pot with 3 liters of distilled water, and 44 lbs (20 kilograms) of brown sugar, or pure granulated sugar cane in large grains.
- Bring very slowly to ebullition, mixing all the time to avoid *rimage* (burn).
- The mixture changes from light gold, to amber, to a warm ebony color, then begins to produce bigger and bigger bubbles—like a volcano. At this precise moment, it is perfect; wait a little longer, and it is spoiled.

Remove it from the fire and add 20 liters of EDV at 60% abv, while always mixing vigorously to dilute the color and un-stick the sides of the pot. Cover immediately to avoid evaporation and loss of alcohol. To make fortified caramel, use one part brut caramel plus two parts EDV at 60% abv. Storage, aging, and racking are identical to syrups.

CHAPTER 19

First manufacture of glass bottles; *La verrerie Claude Boucher à Cognac*, 1904 by René Hérisson

Preparation for Bottling: Adjustment and Filtration

Unlike big companies, which cold-filter their spirits a few times to avoid precipitation due to shipping to various climates, I filter only one time, prior to bottling. Cold filtration makes spirits bright, shiny and more stable, but they are also removing a lot of taste congeners and very good elements of the bouquet. Through trials, one should find the ideal temperature and the tightness necessary to avoid troubles and turbidity in the spirit later, like the appearance of oily droplets or mineral precipitation.

Cold Filtration Procedure

Pump your blend into a stainless steel tank and adjust the alcohol content, color, sweetness, and level of tannins as you think necessary. Remember: all these elements will be lighter after filtration.

Try to be as close as possible to the desired bottling proof of the spirit, and then perform a benchtop (obscuration) distillation in your lab to get a true reading of alcohol percentage. Adjust the alcohol level accordingly. Send a sample to a certified lab for chromatography and make additional adjustments. Remember: the margin allowed is very narrow—between 39.85% abv to 40.00% abv for a spirit with 40% abv printed on the label.

Bring the blend down to 23° F (–5° C), and mix thoroughly to be sure the whole mass is at the proper temperature. Don't touch it for at least 4 or 5 days to allow stabilization (the cold filtration will retain part of the fatty acids and part of their esters of the fatty acids; this is important if you distill the wines with their lees).

Before filtering, rinse the filter medium with pure water to avoid imparting a paper taste. Pump slowly from the racking valve through the filter until the temperature of the spirit going in is identical to that going out. Put these initial gallons to the side to be mixed in the next similar blend.

For clean up filtration, filter medium retention size of 5 to 7 microns should be enough in most cases. For a pristine result, 1 to 3 microns is recommended.

For bottling, the spirit should be at a temperature of 68° F (20° C), for two reasons: To conform to volumetric standards set forth by U.S. and international regulatory law, bottles should be filled precisely with 750 ml at 68° F; and second, this prevents wrinkling of the labels due to condensation. A recovery period of at least three months after filtration and bottling makes the spirit more balanced and harmonious.

Proper proofing methods are detailed in the TTB Gauging Manual (27 CFR Part 30), available online at http://www.ttb.gov/foia/gauging_manual_toc.

Also check the AOAC International website for additional information on production and packaging standards (e.g. for producers intending to export) at www.aoac.org.

CHAPTER 20

Other Wood Species Useful for Flavoring

Below is a glossary of additional wood species useful for flavoring spirits, annotated with generalized tasting characteristics. (Courtesy Black Swan Cooperage.)

Acacia
No tannins; beautiful sweetness.

Cherry
Butter brickle, ripe cherry, fresh grass, meringue and light fried bread/Belgian waffle.

Hard Maple
Maple candy, light spices—nutmeg, cinnamon, syrup, bread/bakery, cream and hint of cocoa.

Hickory (from the walnut family)
Honey, barbecue, hickory smoked bacon, applesauce, cocoa and coconut.

Red Oak
Red berries, toasted marshmallow, light grass, baking bread and butterscotch.

Sassafras

Vanilla, sage/spice, root beer and mint.

Soft Maple

Yellow cake, light smoke, banana, nuts, toasted bread and hint of orange spice.

White Ash

Campfire, marshmallow, light grass, rising bread dough and light sweetness (mouth feel).

White Oak

Vanilla, toasted coconut, cinnamon, pepper, sweet baked bread and caramel.

Yellow Birch

Toffee, butterscotch, honey, croissant, light lemon and tropical fruit.

CHAPTER 21

19th Century barrel reused in Ostbevern, Germany;
photo courtesy Airbnb

Notes on Recycling

Many otherwise discarded byproducts of distillation can be recycled in useful ways. Here are a few suggestions for making use of distillery refuse:

Grape Pommace

Use around the vines and trees. The acetic acid kills weeds and is a good amendment in connection with organic manure and oyster shells.

Stillage

After it is completely cold, the remaining liquid in the still, or "stillage" can be spread between the rows of the vineyards or around fruit trees in the orchards as a fertilizer, on the condition that no chemicals have previously been applied.

Barrels

A few companies are now removing the inside layer (about 5 mm) of spirits barrels without having to take them apart. The barrels then undergo an additional toastage (from light to heavy), made ready for another life.

Tannins

A Russian company is undergoing trials to test oak wood tannins' effectiveness against infestation and diseases in vineyards and orchards.

CHAPTER 22

Artificial Aging

Since the beginning of the 19th century, researchers from around the world have been experimenting with ways to accelerate the aging process of spirits. International legislation forbids all artificial additives to natural EDVs. The purpose here is to discourage distillers from using artificial aging techniques, because they can be detrimental to the quality of the spirit. Some are also illegal—and dangerous. It is necessary to mention them for the sake of scholarship and history, but nothing has yet replaced time and traditional methods of aging: *give time to time.*

1) Champetiers de Cossigny proposed to place EDV in a sealed neutral container (not completely full because of the increase in volume) in boiling water for a few hours.

2) Treatment with wood charcoal is used to increase oxidation and also to absorb some aldehydes.

3) In 1909, Ricciadelli exposed young EDV in a half-full demijohn, tightly closed, in full sun. However, having replicated the experiment myself, I did not find a sensible improvement; but rather an unpleasant dirty smell coming from the fatty congeners.

4) According to De Laparent, the effect of congelation, or

freezing, is equivalent to 12 years in vats. Dr. Lafon from the Station Viticole de Cognac, revisited this experiment by storing Cognac at −274° F (−170° C) in stainless steel containers, placed in liquid nitrogen. Tastings and analysis by sworn tasters did not find a difference between before- or after-experiment samples.

5) Hydrogeneration—According to Kervegant, hydrogen was recommended as able to eliminate unpleasant components of young EDVs, like "greenness." This process was not successful.

6) Treatment by Oxidation—William St. Martin proposed oxygenation under pressure. Before him, in 1892, Villan combined the oxygen under pressure with heat.

Louis Pasteur signaled for the first time in the 1850s the purification effect of ozone on industrial alcohol, but other researchers found it imparted a strong, unpleasant odor to the sample.

7) Catalytic Oxidation—In 1905, Possi-Escot used copper oxide, wood charcoal, and asbestos. Toth, in 1929, tried copper oxide, nickel, and titanium. In 1937, Von Sandor used vanadium, molybdenum, and titanium. Beavens-Goresline and Nelson proposed colloidal silver.

Once again, analysis and tastings found no positive results from these experiments.

8) Radiation and more

Radiation like ultraviolet light, X-rays, and infrared have been tried, along with (in 1942) electric fields, magnetic fields, and ultrasonic vibrations.

9) Electrolysis.

Lasers, microwaves, irradiation absorption, magnets and additives.

All resulted in degradation of the organoleptic characters of the bouquet, loss of length and depth in the spirits.

(From the Bulletin de l'Office International de la Vigne et du Vin, *April 1971. Exposé de Mr. J. Lafon, Station Viticole de Cognac.)*

Tranchage

An old method still used by some producers is *tranchage* (slicing), which consists of slowly bringing up the temperature to 140° F (60° C) for 2 to 3 weeks, with constant circulation of the liquid. Tranchage is usually applied to young EDVs at 70% abv, which are reduced to 65% abv, with *eaux boisés* to speed up integration of the tannins, and then reduced in three steps in vats over 2.5 years.

The experimenters used different temperatures and times. My perception is that the spirit becomes flat and linear and never totally recovers from the shock.

Micro-oxygenation and Clique-age

By introducing low and constant quantities of oxygen into the spirits stored in stainless steel tanks, the micro-oxygenation is supposed to deliver softer tannins for a rounder mouth feel.

With the clique-age, the liquid is saturated with O_2—which is hazardous, overwhelming, and detrimental to organoleptic qualities. Although oxygenation processes are useful and successful for some wines, they do not produce significant positive results with spirits. I personally think some progress can be made using such techniques with fortified *boisés*. In that case, precise time and temperature control, followed by a long resting time in barrels to consume the oxygen, could bring interesting results.

I strongly advocate following international guidelines and legislation to protect appellations. Producers must tell the truth about their spirit production methods, from A to Z. Consumers need to know what they are buying. Labels must warn and protect consumers about methods recognized as nontraditional or otherwise considered manipulative.

CHAPTER 23

Fire Water, or Evil Spirit

Intoxicating liquids have long intrigued people, and were often associated with the divine action from the gods. The Vedic Soma, the Persian Haoma, the ambrosia and the Greek nectar, the hydromel of people from Northern countries, and also the Mexican pulque, are the most significant mythological examples. Their qualities were to thought to bring about immortality. The alchemist Arnaud de Villeneuve mentioned the aqua vitae and its properties of rejuvenation in the 16th century.

The *eau de vie*, also called *aqua ardens* because of its ease of catching fire and ability to produce an internal heat when swallowed, demonstrates the intersection between fire and alcohol.

In Christian societies, EDV was considered to be the invention of evil spirits. Many different stories from central Europe told of the devil teaching distillation to either a peasant or an old woman, who then spread the custom of witchcraft.[1]

---

[1]   Jean-Louis Neveu, Eaux-de-Vie and Bouilleurs, from the *Petite Encyclopedie des Savoirs Populaires.*

CHAPTER 24

Ancient Recipes

Alcohol has been used many different ways to create recipes, and some are original and surprising.

Soap for Shaving

20 grams of white soap, and 80 grams of EDV, melted together in *bain-marie*. After cooling, add some essential oil to perfume it. (From Pierre Poupard)

Cooking

Instead of cutting off the head of poultry, farmers would pour a glass of EDV into their throats, which gave them a heart attack. There are two beneficial effects of this process: First, a happy and gentle end for the animal and, second, the epicurean and initial blending of the blood and the spirit before cooking. It is delicious!

Medicinal Purposes[1]

Colds—To avoid catching a cold after a haircut, rub your entire scalp with a little glass of EDV.

Plague and Cholera—Mix together 2 spoons of goat milk, 2 spoons of sugar, 2 spoons of EDV, 2 spoons of olive olive; stir and drink.

Burns—Infuse a handful of St. John's Wort into a liter of EDV. Gently wash the burned area. Good also for any wounds.

Dysentery and Diarrhea—Drink a glass of EDV, stirred with the yolk of a fresh egg.

Painful Neck—Put black pepper in a cloth, put some EDV on it, and place around the neck.

---

1   From *Le Bienfaiteur de l'Humanité*

CHAPTER 25

Evaluation of the Eaux-De-Vie's Spirituosity

Before Gay-Lussac invented the centesimal alcoholmeter, which in France became obligatory to use on July 8th, 1881, spirit producers had different ways to evaluate the percentage of alcohol.

The first way consisted in impregnating a cloth with the spirit, then light it on fire. The quality of the spirit is judged good when the fabric is consumed by the alcohol.

The second way is to moisten a cannon's powder with the EDV and light it on fire. If the powder does not detonate, the spirit is weak and watery.

The third way is to drip from a certain height a drop of olive oil into the EDV. The depth of the drop's dive gives an indicator of the alcohol content.

Another way is to use dry potash. Pour a small quantity of the EDV on the potash. Depending on how the salt is moistened, the quantity of water in the alcohol may be determined.

Also, to judge the quality of a wine spirit, pour the liquid from a cup at an elevated distance and observe the rounded and loose pearls (bubbles).[1]

---

[1]   From Jean-Louis Neveu, *Eaux de Vie et Bouilleurs, Petite Encyclopedie des Savoirs Populaires.*

CHAPTER 26

The Art of Tasting

"It is difficult to describe an elephant, but when you see one you recognize it immediately."
– Winston Churchill

This analogy represents the difficulty for a taster to put into words the description and the analysis of spirits but, nevertheless, recognize its intrinsic qualities.

The Place
The room should be clean, clear, odorless, quiet, and at a comfortable temperature with natural light. The taster should have a practical way to take notes for his or her examination to avoid distractions.

Health and Life
In order to be at one's optimum sensitivity, the taster should have a healthy life.
- Have regular outdoor activities such as walking, sports, fishing, etc.
- Have enough rest time, both for the body and the mind.
- Eat at regular hours. Food should be balanced—not too spicy nor too hot. Drinks should not be too strong and imbibed in moderation.
- Do not smoke, eat candy, chew gum or drink coffee before tastings.

- Do not use perfumes, aftershave, soap or toothpaste prior to tasting. These will interfere with your judgment and the judgment of other people tasting with you.
- Be truthful in your criticism; the first impression is usually the best.
- Try not to take medicines, or at least very little.
- Taste wines and spirits daily for many years.

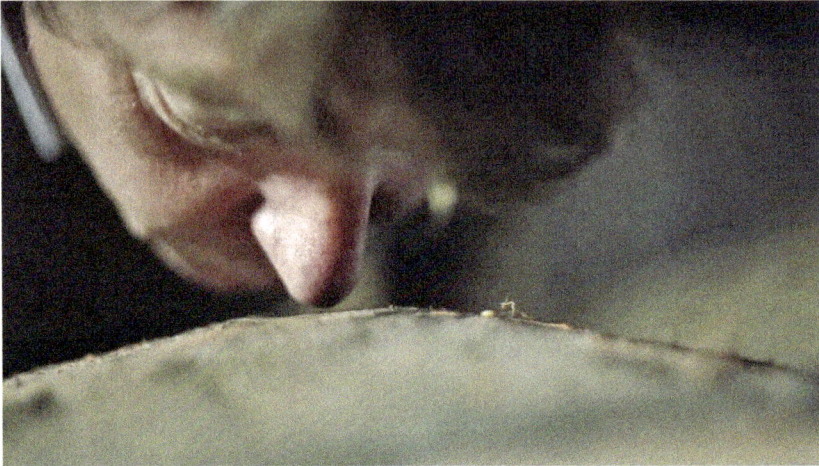

The Cellar Master at work

Sensory Abilities

Heredity—This plays an important role, yet is unquantifiable.

Gender—Tasting is a sensorial and sensual experience, so it is important to open both sides of yourself—your masculinity and femininity, to broaden your perceptions. Nowadays, more women are involved in distillation and blending and bring a precious complement to the evaluation of spirits, consequently in marketing.

Age—Senses weaken with age. Regular tasting helps the taster keep a high level of Efficiency. Long experience compensates for some of the losses in the senses.

Culture and Memory—A good memory and past experiences of odor (good or bad), colors, people, and cultures are constant references for a taster who recollects images, odors and events to identify components. The knowledge of anatomy and descriptive words help the taster share his or her comments. It is important to have good concentration and an open mind when one begins a tasting session.

Mental Approach

Slow down before evaluating samples. Organize your brain in order to concentrate on one category of smell at a time and in a certain order.

Create mental categories to focus upon. The tasting is more descriptive and poetic if the focus is on fruits, flowers, spices and other fragrances. Perform a structural analysis about length, depth, balance, harmony and complexity. The characters of aging potential, weakness and defects require steady and regular evaluation.

To dive deeper into yourself and into the samples, redo your tasting with your eyes closed. The increased level of perception and complexity will surprise you. Some obscure details become more apparent. Why is that? "While the visual areas of the brain are active, other areas involved with smell, taste, and touch are largely shut down."
—Michio Kaku, *The Future of the Mind*

Switching Exercises—Change from one subject to another, but always take a few seconds to rest, to be more efficient and to save the acuity of your nose. With time and experience, you will be the *driver* of your nose and brain and will not get lost in details and description (you can always come back to them). You will feel the prime importance of the frame and the construction of your product.

When to Taste

The most valuable time of the day is in the morning from 9 am to noon, when your senses are well rested and your appetite is growing. You are more alert, more sensitive, and have an acute sense of smell. Springtime is also a better time to taste, after the spirits have been dormant during the winter.

Important: Both the samples and the taster should be at room temperature.

The Tasting Glasses

Tulip shape closed has a base slightly wider than the opening of the glass. Tulip shape opened is egg-shaped with a taper at the mouth. Experts recommend both glasses; they favor the rising sensation of the aromas and reveal the finesse and delicateness of the spirits.

The "cellar master" glass has straight sides, and allows aroma to rise directly into the nose, showing finesse and subtlety of the spirit.

The Sniffer, or Liar—Never use balloon glasses of any size (the bigger, the worse) because the aggression of the alcohol flattens the senses, taking away all the finesse and complexity of the spirits.

Wash tasting glasses by hand with hot water only—absolutely no detergent—and let them air dry on a rack. Do not put them on a cloth.

To avoid being influenced by the color of spirits, Master Tasters use cellar master glasses, which are blue, black or golden in color.

[left to right] tulip glass, the sniffer or liar, and the "cellar master" glass; courtesy L'Amateur-Cognac

Blue glasses; courtesy L'Amateur-Cognac

Judging

Pour one fluid ounce of liquid into the glass. Consistency is important to fairly judge the color, the rising sensation, and the intensity.

Visual Examination—By holding the glass by the foot and tilting it against a white background or light, the judge looks at the clarity, viscosity, and color. The sample should not be cloudy nor have sediments. Depending on its age, kind of oak, and toastage, the spirits should reveal a multitude of different hues, ranging from pale yellow to dark amber.

Odor—This is the direct olfactory sensation experienced when you smell the liquid without any movement and at different distances from the glass to evaluate the intensity. Rotate the liquid in the glass to increase aeration, releasing more aromatic components.

Aroma—This is the indirect olfactory sensation produced by drinking the liquid. Perception in the back of the mouth and back in your nose is called retro-olfaction. Just a few drops are necessary with aeration, so the liquid is in contact with all the taste receptors of the mouth (5 to 10 seconds maximum, then reject the liquid).

Evaluate the length, aromatic character, and the flavors (nose and mouth). Good spirits should give good sensations for at least 30 seconds after swallowing them.

Taste—Many direct sensations are perceived in the mouth. The tongue perceives taste according to distinct locations of tastebuds: Sugar at the tip of the tongue, acid on both sides, salt in the middle, and bitter at the very back of the tongue. Temperature and spiciness play an important role in evaluating the balance between softness, acidity, bitterness, roundness, body, oiliness, and volume.

There are also indirect sensations perceived in the mouth. Umami is a savory taste detected on the tongue and other regions of the mouth coming from the chemical compound glutamate. A taste for fats, or "oleogustus" brings up the taste of food, wine and spirits. Wine distilled with the lees or produced using malolactic fermentation gives complexity and length to spirits.

The palate underlines the nose by affirmation or infirmation.

Bouquet—Evaluation of the synthesis of the odors (direct) and aromas (indirect) for complexity, balance, finesse and elegance.

Body—Round and consistent impression on the palate. The spirit is smooth and suave as opposed to dry and flat.

Dry—A spirit that is neither sweet nor smooth.

Flavor—Combination of sensations in the nose and the mouth (taste plus bouquet).

Length—Quality of a spirit of which the bouquet and smoothness remain a long time in the nose and the mouth.

Montant—Rising sensations, or the first sensations released by the spirit.

Robe, or dress—Color of the spirit.

Savour—Sensation of taste on the tongue and palate.

Characteristic to note: Classification of odor and fragrances are quite subjective and provisional.

- General: Appearance, volatility, intensity, depth, and length.
- Particularity: Aromatics, flavors, complexity, and structure.
- Finish: Harmony, balance, elegance, finesse, and delicateness.

Tasting and blending require a pattern of recognition between the aromas instead of pure memorization.

Additional Techniques

Dilution—By cutting a higher proof spirit to about 40% abv with warm distilled water, you make them more approachable.

Add the water slowly, swirling the glass at the same time to avoid saponification of the liquid. As a distiller and a master blender, this helps me detect the defects and their origins (either from the ingredients, fermentation, distillation, maturation, or filtration). Hidden qualities are revealed by a slight dilution of high proof spirits.

Gentle Approaches—When a spirit is either strong in alcohol or aggressive, smell at the top of the glass above the rim and slightly open your mouth. The result is a much softer spirit with less attack.

Bottom of the Glass—At the end of my tastings, I empty the glasses and cover them with glass covers (no papers or cardboard), and come back to note my impression after a few hours, days or, sometimes, even weeks. It reveals the intensity, the power and the true character; especially, but not only, for aged spirits that have acquired nutty, leathery, and spicy balsamic flavors of rancio.

Recovering Between Sample Tasting:

A technique used by perfumers: Take a cotton ball, open it and breathe through your nose to absorb and neutralize the odors. Generally speaking, we said that the nose is able to smell a maximum of 3 to 5 odors at a time.

Another technique is to smell the inside of your elbow. The importance is to smell a neutral or familiar odor such as your own body odor.

The Origins of Aromas

Primary Aromas

The skin and the pulp are where the aromatic substances of fruit, flowers, and spices reside. They are influenced by the varietal, nature of the soil, and the microclimate. Due to the fragility of the components, it is important to avoid oxidation of the must and have a clean fermentation.

Secondary Aromas

The alcoholic fermentation of the sugar creates alcohols, aldehydes, volatile acids, esters, and acetates. Malolactic fermentation brings creamy or buttery tastes and gives more length and mouth feel. Both come into play and add to the complexity of the liquid.

Tertiary Aromas

With the extraction of components from the wood, the organoleptic characteristics go through a transformation. During aging, you notice a small diminution of the primary elements and an important modification of the secondary components. With time and oxidation, the bouquet gains subtlety and complexity.

Defects and Their Origins

During the first part of the aging process, defects can appear whose consequences could be important. They also tend to increase with time.

Bitterness—Coming from an excess of tannins in oak that was not seasoned long enough, or of poor quality, ruining the bouquet and finesse.

Rancid—Due to used barrels in bad shape or which previously contained defective EDVs, heads, tails, or wines.

Sap and Varnish—Coming from the sapwood of oak or another type of wood.

Oxidation—During aging, spirits go through a period of oxidation due to the digestion of the tannins. It is NOT a defect, but a temporary characteristic, preceding another level of maturity.

Aromas Chart

Wheel labels:

Outer ring: APPLE, PEAR, LEMON, GRAPEFRUIT, ORANGE, LIME, GOOSEBERRY, GRAPE, PINEAPPLE, MELON, BANANA, PEACH, APRICOT, MANGO, LYCHEE, CHERRY, STRAWBERRY, RASPBERRY, PLUM, BLACKBERRY, BLACKCURRANT, RAISIN, PRUNE, FIG, JAM, CHOCOLATE, TOFFEE, BUTTERSCOTCH, HONEY, VANILLA, CEDAR, OAK, SMOKE, TOBACCO, LIQUORICE, PEPPER, CINNAMON, GROUND COFFEE, LEATHER, BACON, GAME, TRUFFLES, EUCALYPTUS, MINT, GREEN PEPPER, ASPARAGUS, CUT GRASS, HAY, BLOSSOM, ELDERFLOWERS, RED ROSES, VIOLETS, ALMONDS, BISCUITS, GRILLED NUTS, TOAST, BREAD, YEAST, CREAM, BUTTER, PETROL, EARTH, STONES, FLINT

Inner ring: FRUITY, MINERAL, DAIRY, NUTTY, FLORAL, HERBAL, SAVOURY, SPICE, WOOD, SWEET

Center: WINE NOT

ODOR:
The objective of the olfactory examination is to judge the intensity, complexity and quality of a wine's aroma, and subsequently to identify and describe the character of the specific odors of which it is composed. The sense of smell is the key to enjoying wine, because it enables us to perceive both aroma and subtleties of flavor.

COMPLEXITY:
Term for wine exhibiting depth of aromas, and variety of odorous sensations after being inhaled.

INTENSITY:
is made up of various odorous sensations coming together at once. Is a measure of quantity and not necessarily quality: in a fine wine an intense bouquet is an attribute but in a poor quality wine a strong odour can be a negative factor.

QUALITY:
Represents the synthesis relating both to olfactory intensity and complexity, as well as finesse, elegance, frankness and tepidity. The taster's experience and knowledge of wines play an important role in the evaluation of the olfactory quality.

Courtesy: Gossip Chef

Oak Aroma Chart

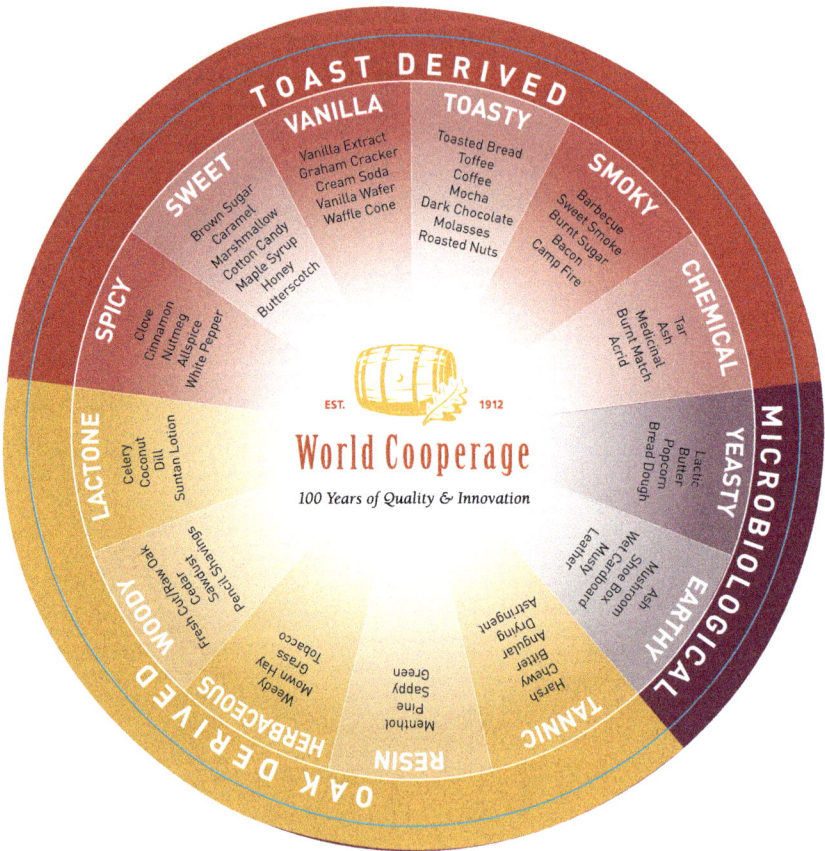

Courtesy: World Copperages

CHAPTER 27

Conclusion

Through aging options and maturation steps described throughout this book, choices can be made in harmony with your own geographic and financial situations. They will determine your goals and influence the quality of your spirits and their places in the market.

By digesting the know-how of the previous spirits masters and turning yourself toward the future, you will gain momentum; yet, be aware of your brain—it is more powerful and tricky than you can imagine.

Aging spirits is primarily a game of patience, where vision and experience nurture your confidence to make the right decisions. Even after many years of work and research, you always learn new ways and details to improve quality. Understanding other people's products will generate new ideas. Changing yourself will refine your art and nourish your passion. Discover the painter, the musician, the dancer, the artist—the distiller you dream of being by keeping yourself on the edge and not falling into a comfortable routine where seeming expertise makes you sleepy, inattentive and bumptious. One just has to have an open, determined, and curious mind by staying in touch with the past and turning to the future.

Remember these words from Albert Einstein: "The true sign of intelligence is not knowledge but imagination."

Thoughts and News

Sounds of someone's name or the color of the room can influence behaviors and thoughts.

Our environment shapes our thoughts and actions in myriad ways without our permission or even our knowledge. Colors influence our mood; how sunny days can induce optimism as well as aggression. Curved furnishings and red lighting makes single malts taste sweeter.

The restaurant Ultraviolet, in Shanghai, pairs each dish on the 20-course menu with kaleidoscopic wall projections, computerized lighting, scent diffusions and surround sound—all to intensify the taste of food (from *The Telegraph*, Feb. 15, 2015). There is development of "electronic tongues" which use sensors to measure taste and smell—an ideal way to try before you buy. The E-delicious Machine, unveiled by the Thai government in September 2014, is a good example, intended to safeguard against unwittingly consuming poorly made food or drinks.

Future

In the future, what will be the role and the influence of the master distiller and the master blender to their art? Will technology replace us by offering shortcuts and programs of punctual data, reducing creativity to only a purely theoretical view?

It is only a matter of time before we can insert artificial memories into our brains, to learn new subjects and master new hobbies. One day, scientists might construct an "internet of the mind" or a brain-net, where thoughts and emotion are sent electronically around the world. Even dreams will be videotaped and "brain-mailed" across the Internet.

(Michio Kaku, *The Future of the Mind*)

Bouquet of Olfactory Thoughts

"When the scents are colors and the colors become scents."
—HGR

"The piano of the heart and the violins of the soul."
—Léo Ferré

"While other spirits sail on symphonies, mine, my beloved swims along your scent."
—Charles Baudelaire

"The one who lost himself in his passion is loosing less than the one who lost his passion." —St. Augustine

"The future belongs to those who believe in the beauty of their dreams."
—Eleanor Roosevelt

APPENDICES

METRIC CONVERSIONS

LENGTH
1 centimeter = 10 millimeters (mm)
1 inch = 2.54 centimeters (cm)
1 foot = 0.3048 meters (m)
1 yard = 3 feet
1 meter (m) = 100 centimeters (cm)
1 meter (m) = 3.280839895 feet
1 furlong = 660 feet
1 kilometer (km) = 1000 meters (m)
1 kilometer (km) = 0.62137119 miles
1 mile = 5280 feet
1 mile = 1.609344 kilometers (km)
1 nautical mile = 1.852 kilometers (km)

AREA
1 square foot = 144 square inches
1 square foot = 929.0304 square centimeters
1 square yard = 9 square feet
1 square meter = 10.7639104 square feet
1 acre = 43,560 square feet
1 hectare = 2.4710538 acres
1 square kilometer = 100 hectares
1 square mile = 2.58998811 square kilometers
1 square mile = 640 acres

VOLUME
1 US tablespoon = 3 US teaspoons
1 US fluid ounce = 29.57353 milliliters (ml)
1 US cup = 16 US tablespoons
1 US cup = 8 US fluid ounces
1 US pint = 2 US cups
1 US pint = 16 US fluid ounces
1 liter (l) = 33.8140227 US fluid ounces
1 liter (l) = 1000 milliliters (ml)
1 US quart = 2 US pints
I US gallon = 4 US quarts
1 US gallon = 3.78541178 liters

WEIGHT
1 milligram (mg) = 0.001 grams (g)
1 gram (g) = 0.001 kilograms (kg)
1 gram (g) = 0.035273962 ounces
1 ounce = 28.34952312 grams (g)
1 ounce = 0.0625 pounds
1 pound (lb) = 16 ounces
1 pound (lb) = 0.45359237 kilograms (kg)
1 kilogram (kg) = 35.273962 ounces
1 kilogram (kg) = 2.20462262 pounds (lb)
1 stone = 14 pounds
1 short ton = 2000 pounds
1 metric ton = 1000 kilograms (kg)

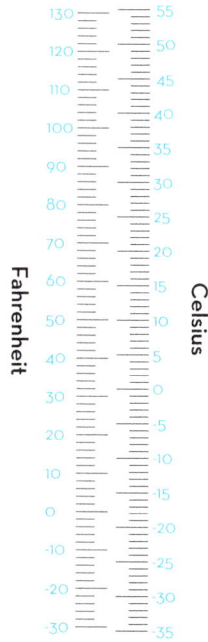

Fahrenheit / **Celsius** temperature scale

Fahrenheit	Celsius
130	55
120	50
110	45
100	40
90	35
80	30
70	25
60	20
50	15
40	10
30	5
20	0
10	-5
0	-10
-10	-15
-20	-20
-30	-25
	-30
	-35

Glossary

Alembic or alambic A pot still made in cognac that has a well-designed shape and appropriate dimensions. The hat and swan neck size are particularly important to quality.

Angels' share The most common expression for the evaporation of spirits through the staves of a barrel. Different names are used in various regions and countries of the world.

Bending or arching Fr. *cintrage;* heat and water are applied to progressively bend the staves together to form the rounded shape of the barrel.

Blending *Assemblage* of different years, varietals or vineyards to obtain balance, complexity and consistency

Boises An aqueous extract of oak containing concentrated wood tannins. They should be fortified for conservation and aging.

Bolt Fr. *billon*, or block, split following the modular ray of the wood.

Brix Measure of the sugar content in fruits and grapes.

Cellar Fr. *chai*, aging cellar

Coarse grain Fast or summer growth wood.

Furfural Caramelization produced from wood sugars and a marker for heavier, toasty flavors.

Grove Fr. *rognage;* preparation consisting of trimming the bottom and the ends of the staves to fit the heads of barrels.

Hydrolis Conversion by reaction with water: either the breakdown of oak tannins during seasoning, or the breakdown of esters during maturation into less flavorsome acids and alcohols.

Maderisation Process that involves the heating and oxidation of components in wines and spririts.

Oak extract *see* Boises

Oxidation Breathing through the staves, oxygen produces acetyl and generates delicate fragances (pleasant or not). During pumping and blending, oxygen also changes the structure of the tannins, altering color and flavors.

Proof A measure of alcohol by volume. (In the U.S. it is calculated by doubling the ABV percentage.)

Raising Fr. *elevage*, a term used when spirits are brought to maturity.

Rancio Nutty, leathery or balsamic flavors developing after many years of aging.

Rimage (burn Resulting from heavy solids or high heat at one spot in the pot still.

Ring Fr. *cerne*, annular growth structures in wood that are used to determine the age of the tree.

Saponification Due to a fast and abrupt reduction with water the spirit becomes cloudy and tastes soapy. It is more accentuated when distillation occurs with more congeners.

Seasoning Fr. *sechage*; during a period of 2 to 3 years outside in open work stacks, boards go through important changes: reduction of moisture from 90% to ~15%, loss of the astringent and bitter tannins, oxidation of the tannins in polyphenols and degradation of the lignin with oxidation of the aldehydes and phenolic acid

Staves Fr. *douelles*; after seasoning, the boards are mechanically worked into a cylindrical shape, curved and trimmed to the right length to become staves.

Tannins Polyphenols present in wood and vegetative matter that break down in the presence of water. A spirit that has aged for too long in a new cask has an excess of tannins, a flaw that renders it undrinkable due to its bitterness and astringency.

Terroir Not always a quality factor. Arises from the growing conditions (soils, elevation, micro-climate). Of all the ingredients, it can bring an unpleasant taste that is rough and bitter. Too much "terroir" is detrimental to the fineness and delicateness of the aromas.

Toastage Fr. *bousinage*; by turning open barrels over a source of heat for various lengths of time and intensity, you obtain the desired toastage.

Water of life Fr. *eau-de-vie*; clear, unaged spirit made from grapes or fruits.

Acknowledgments

With my best thanks...

My wife Carole and my sons Alex and Raphael, for their patience and their love during my constant researching through a never-ending story.

Nancy Frawley, for her passion and immortal enthusiasm in the quest for quality and authenticity in the worlds of spirits.

Drew Faulkner, for his appetite and true appreciation of premium spirits. He brought common sense and the "American" vision to this book.

Gail Sands, for her artistic eyes and her creativity. They were precious assets in the illustration of this book.

Bill Owens, for his trust and loyalty in helping me share my desire to help fellow craft distillers fulfill their dreams.

Brad Plummer, for his keen sense of detail in the finishing part of editing.

Richard Braastad, Cellar Master at Tiffon /Braastad cognac, for his long complicity and true passion for epicurean spirits.

Jean-Paul Margot, Master Distiller at Hennessy Cognac. His friendship has been and is still essential in giving me confidence and strength through the achievement of this book. Working and experimenting together for many years has been an enriching experience.

To all my friends on both sides of the "pond", who believed and supported me during all these years.

Marcel Jacqueton, Cellar Master at Jules Robin Cognac, who kept an eye on me since my birth in the hope that I will eventually join the circle of cellar masters. His sense of reality and his simplicity have been a precious inspiration in my journey.

Pierre-Alain Gardrat, Master Taster at the Organisation Economique du Cognac, for opening my senses and educating my palate in weekly sessions, which greatly elevated my ability to taste and to appreciate cognacs.

Pierre Frugier, Master Blender at Martell Cognac, for allowing me to freely explore all aspects of the aging process during my apprenticeship at the Cognac Martell house.

Jean, Jean-Louis, Jean-Charles Vicard of Tonnellerie Vicard, for providing advise since the early eighties, in addition to all types of seasoned barrels during my research in matching grapes varietals and tannin potentials.

CPSIA information can be obtained at www.ICGtesting.com
Printed in the USA
BVOW05*1953170716

455877BV00003B/3/P